———————— About the Author ————————

John Bligh was born in London in 1922. Post-war, he studied Physiology at University College London, and received the University of London degrees of Ph.D. (1952) and DSc (1977). He is a Fellow of the Institute of Biology (UK), and has received an honorary LL.D. degree from the Simon Fraser University, British Columbia (Canada). He advanced to Senior Principal Scientific Officer in the service of the UK Agricultural Research Council, before ending his research career as Director of the Institute of Arctic Biology and Professor of Physiology at the University of Alaska, Fairbanks. His interests have been divided between physiological researches, thirty years of service on governing bodies of Cambridgeshire schools, and the matters considered here.

THE FATAL INHERITANCE

THE FATAL INHERITANCE

John Bligh

ATHENA PRESS
LONDON

First Published 2004 by
ATHENA PRESS
Queen's House, 2 Holly Road
Twickenham TW1 4EG
United Kingdom

Printed for Athena Press

The problem of the natural relationship between populations and food supplies, and features of our inherited natures, from which it is so hard to escape...

John Bligh

I tell you naught for your comfort
Yea, naught for your desire
Save that the sky grows darker yet
And the sea rises higher.

G K Chesterton

ACKNOWLEDGEMENTS

Helpful discussants and discussions over the years are too numerous for all to be remembered and named. My thanks, if they remember, and my apologies if some should feel slighted. I am especially grateful to Dr Victor Whittaker (an erstwhile research colleague) for his perusal of the nearly finished text, and his valued advice; and to my colleague, Professor Dr Renate Hanitzsch, at the Carl Ludwig Institute of Physiology (Leipzig University) for her tremendous and diligent help in bringing this task to its conclusion. Thanks also to Mr B Bartsch of that Institute, and my son, Peter Bligh, for help with the preparation of the figures and text. Also, thanks to my wife for tolerating my obsession for so long.

CONTENTS

A SYNOPTIC PREFACE

There were six billion of us in the year 2000, which compares with less than 2 billion in the year 1900, and less than 1 billion in the year 1800. This massive inflation of human numbers over the last two hundred years, and the last hundred years particularly, underlies virtually all that ails mankind today. Without such unnaturally inflated numbers of Homo sapiens, doing what all animals do, but more cleverly and effectively so, there would be no soil pollution or exhaustion, no shortages of potable water, no over-exploitation of the materials of the Earth's crust, no emptying of the seas of fishes, and none of the other pollutions of land, sea and atmosphere now occurring, and threatening not only the survival of many species of fauna and flora, but ultimately of Homo sapiens itself.

In all animals the primary endeavours are self-preservation and reproduction. Reproduction needs only opportunity to be carried to a greater extent than the available food supply can sustain into maturity. Self-preservation is achieved by securing, if necessary by aggression, food enough for oneself and one's still immature progeny. Premature death of progeny in excess of feedability is inevitable. It is this that effects the equation of food supplies and numbers, aided by the mortality of intra-species and inter-species conflicts over territory and food supplies. For all its vanity, Homo sapiens is no different from others of the animal kingdom except in this one respect: its exceptional ability to progressively increase its understanding and exploitation of its environment. The codification of that understanding is labelled *science*; its application to environmental exploitation, control and usage, divides into agriculture, medicine and industry. Industrial progress provides both the material comforts of human lifestyles and improved abilities to wage war. Medical advancements increase the prospects of longevity; while agricultural advancements allow ever more Homo sapiens to be extant at any time, and to engage in conflict over food supplies and other coveted materials. Since reproduction, uncontrolled, is the relentless provider of humans seeking to survive, it is the limitation of the food supply that is, directly or indirectly, the principal determinant of population size, with the inequitable distribution of the food supply serving as an additional check. The inevitable consequence of unrestrained reproduction, then, is that there will always be hunger, and consequential premature death, for a proportion of humanity, irrespective of the extent of the food supply. That proportion has probably remained more or less constant as the total human population has risen. Therefore the numbers of hungry persons and premature deaths has also risen.

Whatever one may believe concerning a supernatural involvement in procreation, and in the responsibility for the supply of the wants of others, it is likely that nothing but our own endeavours can stem the progress of the species towards the day when overstretched agriculture peaks and then collapses, and/or the environments becomes so intolerably polluted, that a human population crash occurs. Such a disaster would almost certainly provoke bitter conflicts over possession of what means of survival remain. In the meantime, hunger and premature death will remain the controller of population sizes, whatever can be achieved agriculturally, and whatever the scale of relief that can be brought to regions where hunger is greatest.

This destiny of mankind is not, however, wholly unavoidable. There is one escape route, which is the urgent and sustained containment of human population size. Either we act to adjust our numbers to whatever the maximum sustainable food supply may be, and thereby spare much human suffering, or the food supply will continue to adjust our numbers, but with much avoidable suffering. The choice is ours.

Chapter One

MY LONG-STANDING CONCERN: A PERSONAL PROLOGUE

My own concern over the problem of equating the increasing human population with the ability to feed everyone started more than fifty years ago. In 1942, being to my chagrin no longer considered fit enough to die in combat, I was duly shorn of the uniformed respectability of the war years. Hoping to be still useful, I found employment as a very junior research assistant at Britain's National Institute for Medical Research. There I became involved in one, and aware of the other, of two seminal developments that were ultimately to have far greater impacts upon mankind than was the outcome of World War II itself. One was the introduction into clinical usage of penicillin. This was the first of the organismic extracts which fulfilled the hope of the pioneer microbiologist, Paul Ehrlich (1854–1915), that there could be a 'golden bullet' that, while harmless to humans when introduced into their bodies, could destroy invading pathogenic micro-organisms. Why penicillin was inappropriately described as an 'antibiotic' agent – meaning 'against life' without qualification – rather than 'antimicrobiotic', is not clear. It was soon evident that penicillin, and the several other subsequently discovered organismic exudates with somewhat similar properties, could be 'pro-biotic' (i.e. for life) for mankind.

My own very minor involvement in the emerging saga of the antibiotic era was to assist in the biological standardisation of what was then a quite dirty extraction from the medium in which the mould *Penicillium notatum* had been incubated. The other development at that time was the start of the mass use of the first of the industrially synthesised insecticides, DDT (dichlorodiphenyltrichloroethane), which is lethal to the insect vectors of such micropathogens as those causing typhus and malaria, but which was then considered to be relatively harmless to humans if inhaled. DDT was used successfully on a massive scale in 1944 when Naples was first occupied by the Allied armies, and found to be in the midst of a typhus epidemic. In succeeding years DDT was used extensively to destroy the malaria parasite-bearing mosquito.

It has been estimated that before the introduction of penicillin and DDT, a quarter of all human deaths worldwide was directly or indirectly attributable to the mosquito-borne malarial parasite; and that about half of all deaths worldwide was the consequence of microbial infections generally. Death in old age, largely attributable to the accumulation of genetic errors in the somatic (non-reproductive) cells of the body, was the good fortune of only a small minority of human beings. It was evident, even as these developments were being applied on a still quite small scale, that their widespread availability would cause a major imbalance between the occurrences of births and deaths. Since the imbalance was entirely in the direction of the extension of lifetimes which, had natural biological interactions been allowed to proceed, would have been terminated much earlier, the consequence would be an increase in populations. Furthermore, since many of these extended lives would otherwise have been terminated before the attainment of sexual maturity, there would be a progressive increase in the numbers of mating pairs. Thus there would be an increase in the birth rate from generation to generation, as well as an increase in life expectancy. Between them, all these interferences with the natural interplay between living organisms had the propensity of producing a human population explosion on a scale hitherto unknown in the history of Homo sapiens.

These advances in medicine and public health promised to 'save lives' on an unprecedented scale, and were heralded as triumphs, but some of those engaged in the basic and applied aspects of these new weapons against microbial diseases were quick to realise that 'saving lives' and 'sustaining lives' are two independent operations. The one largely depends upon medical interventions, but the other depends upon the adequacy of the food supply. Unless the food supply could be increased in line with the population increase, these medical triumphs could quickly turn sour as premature death by infection is replaced by premature death by starvation. Indeed it seems possible that Alexander Fleming, who in 1928 had observed the anti-bacterial effect of a *Penicillium notatum* mould found to be growing on the agar of a Petri dish which had been seeded with the pathogenic micro-organism *staphylococcus aureus,* was aware of this and is said to have remarked years later, after the extract, penicillin, had been put into clinical usage, that in time the world would curse him for his observation. The implication of that remark, if really said by Fleming, was that such a massive interference with the balance between births and death would inevitably exacerbate the already existing problem of producing enough food for everyone.

Medical researchers and practitioners do not generally concern themselves greatly with the demographic, social, political and nutritional consequences of their own endeavours to overcome all causes of death before extreme old age. The success in their endeavours is reward enough, and any consequential problems are for others to resolve. In about 1945, however, I happened to overhear a discussion over lunch amongst senior colleagues at the National Institute for Medical Research, on what might happen when the clinical use of antibiotics substantially reduced the incidence of premature deaths. Could the human population expand dramatically in consequence in a country such as the United Kingdom that, still largely deprived of food imports, was already hard-pressed to produce enough food to sustain its present population?

The question seemed largely academic at that time, and certainly could not be brought to the immediate attention of a wider audience. The possibility of a medicine-induced famine in the years ahead was not a matter to be considered at a time when there was still a war, and a peace, to be won. This conversation, however, stayed imprinted on my mind. Thus when, in 1946, I went to University College, London, to study physiology with the intention of pursuing a career in medical research, I continued to take note of a slowly increasing concern over the growing problem of whether enough food could be produced to sustain the burgeoning human population of the world. Because of this persistent concern, I decided to apply myself to agriculturally-related research rather than to medically-related research. I well remember the looks of amusement and disbelief of a group of medical students I was tutoring, when I first ventured the opinion that with the control of malaria, tuberculosis and other infectious diseases, starvation could become the most prevalent cause of death, and that no medicine would then be able to alleviate the sufferings of hunger, and prevent an early death.

The earliest of the pamphlets and newspaper cuttings on matters of population and food supplies which I collected in the 1940s and 1950s is a discussion paper, 'Problems of Population' by Titmuss (1942), who recognised that the rapid increase of the world's population, which had begun around 1600 CE, and had been gathering pace ever since, would become a matter of increasing concern once World War II was over and other world problems could again be addressed. Titmuss's apprehension, however, was not about the equation of global numbers of humans and global food supplies. His concern was that since the populations of some countries were growing faster than those of others, and that in some instances the growth was being encouraged by political and/or religious leaders, these regional population changes could affect the balances of international power, and could become threats to the integrity and safety of other regions or nations. In this context he related an alleged conversation between Napoleon and Madame de Stael in which de Stael asked Napoleon whom he considered to be the greatest woman. 'She, madam,' he replied, 'who furnishes the most cannon fodder at her country's need.' Manpower was, and to some extent still is, crucial both for the successful execution of aggression, and for successful defence against aggression. Thus when a potential enemy is growing stronger and larger, there is inevitable concern that a threatened state should have manpower enough to defend itself.

At an International Congress on Population and World Health Resources in relation to the Family in 1948, the concern was with peripheral social issues rather than the central, but still only vaguely recognised, issue of the equation of world food production and world population. A year later, however, in a UNESCO-sponsored current affairs pamphlet, Aldous Huxley (1949) clearly identified the equation of world population and world food supplies as the fundamental issue that underlay all the better-recognised social and political considerations. He dissented from a prevailing view that resources would be adequate for any foreseeable increase in the world population, and that the only real problems for mankind were the inefficiencies of food production, and the inequitable distribution of harvests. A particular concern of Huxley was that efforts to compel the soil to yield the ever greater harvests needed to feed a continuously increasing human population, would ultimately result in massive soil erosion, which could have disastrous consequences for a numerically much enlarged human population. This was, it seems, the first intimation of the inability of the terrestrial surfaces of the world to produce an ever-increasing amount of food to supply the needs of an ever-increasing human population. At some point the soil could become exhausted, and food production would start to decline. A human population crash would then become inevitable.

A co-contributor to that pamphlet was the agriculturist John Russell (1949), who was more optimistic. Life, he observed, had always been hard for most of mankind, and would continue to be. He believed, however, that with courage, intelligence and an unconquerable faith (whatever that means), mankind would be able to overcome whatever difficulties an increasing world population might cause. He emphasised the impossibility of setting any upper limit to the world's food resources, and stated that so long as food production per agricultural worker, and per acre, increased as populations increased, there would be no food crisis.

The delegates at a world Population Congress which took place in Rome in 1954, many of whom were doctrinally opposed to any form of birth control, largely succeeded in assuring themselves that Russell was right, and that Mother Earth could provide food enough for whatever increase in populations might occur. Considering the near exponential rate of increase in the number of mouths to feed, and the finite amount of land suitable for agriculture, this would seem to have been an utterly irrational faith in what agricultural science could achieve, and/or an equally irrational faith in what prayer could achieve. Not everyone was equally convinced of the possibility of increasing food supplies in line with population increases indefinitely. It was felt by some that the wisest approach would be to be less optimistic, and to seek ways to both maximise sustainable agricultural productivity and at the same time to minimise the rate of growth of the human population. Indeed, both India and Japan had by then already adopted population limitation policies as preferable to the risk of mass starvation.

No rational being could believe that an exponential rise in food production would be able to follow an exponential rise in population indefinitely. A slowing-down of the rate of population increase, and its eventual stabilisation at a sustainable level, was manifestly the only way to eliminate the risk of an ultimate disaster. A worldwide encouragement of contraception was an obvious and necessary precaution against a failure to equate population and food production, and all the unimaginable distress that would then follow. Too many delegates attending the 1954 congress in Rome chose to believe otherwise.

For once the delegates from the Vatican and the USSR were united in their opposition to engineered population limitations. The Catholics, perhaps with an awareness of the enormity of the suffering that their dogma on this issue could cause, cautiously refrained from absolute opposition to family planning. When pregnancy was not the objective, the Church would only sanction natural sexual intercourse in the so-called 'safe period'. At other times strictly observed coitus reservatus, was deemed permissible but with coitus interruptus reserved for unintended 'emergency circumstances'. The Soviet delegate argued only that the proper course was to increase food production as the needs of a growing human population increased, and to leave pregnancy unhindered. Food production, he declared, could be increased, as and when needed. This, he said, could be done, as was evident from the historical experience of the Soviet Union. In point of fact, following the Soviet agrarian reform, which Stalin once told

Churchill, had cost some six million lives, the Soviet Union never succeeded in producing all the food it needed, and was later only able to avoid disastrous food shortages by importing grain from North America. Thus there was little objectivity, little sense, and little progress in Rome in 1954. Creeds, both theological and political, were united in their opposition to any progress being made towards a rational response to an increasing problem.

Commenting on this pathetic assembly, Nicholson (1954) complained that the delegates had spared no attention to the vast and menacing explosion of the human population, which medical progress had detonated. He pointed out that an FAO survey had reported that already at that time 1,750 million of the world's 3,000 million human population – that is, more than 50% – suffered hunger for at least part of every year. This hunger was mostly in countries where the expansion of food production to match population rises was low or non-existent. Sadly prophetically, Nicholson asked, 'Will famine in bad years, now often narrowly averted, reach such a scale as to nullify the progress in death control resulting from medical research?' He added that when the balancing of death control with birth control is finally recognised as the most crucial issue facing mankind, leaders of religious sects may need to be told that they bear an even greater responsibility than that of governments for a mountain of avoidable human suffering that could far outstrip the inhumanities of Stalin and Hitler combined. Nicholson asked, 'Is it defensible to shower money on research for preventing deaths, and also for hydrogen bombs, but assiduously to neglect research which might, in time, help to prevent world tensions from becoming uncontrollable, and hydrogen bombs from being used?'

A year later (1955), in a Political and Economic Planning report on world population and resources, it was pointed out that inequalities in population densities, in health and happiness, in food and material supplies, and in much else besides, are likely to become greater as time passes, unless the growth of populations in the overcrowded countries is somehow restrained. The report acknowledged that the increase in world food production was then outstripping that of population, but noted that the increase in food production was mainly in countries in which the additional food was least needed.

It is evident, then, that nearly half a century ago, it was clearly understood by those who cared to consider the matter, that the total human population of the world was growing at an increasing rate; and that without either an increase in food production at a comparable rate, or a limitation in the rate of the increase in human numbers, a disastrous situation would arise sooner or later. The already high level of malnutrition worldwide, would become even greater. Hunger would lead to intertribal strife, and in a new age of potential mass destruction by nuclear weaponry, tribal strife could lead to annihilation.

In the early 1950s it was evident that food production could be increased to some extent by the maximisation of land usage, the selection of high yielding crops, and efficient land management. Even so, however, common sense should have counselled that the continuously expanding food production needed to supply the needs of an unlimited exponential growth of population could at best be sustained for only a limited time, and perhaps for only a very limited time. The apparent notion that an exponential increase in food production could allow an exponential increase in the human population indefinitely was patently absurd. Lewis (1957) pointed out that if the world population doubled every 25 years, which was approximately the time it was estimated that it would take for the population in 1957 to double, then by the year 2330 CE there would be 173,500 billion extant human beings. There would then be standing room only because, Lewis stated, there is that number of square yards of land surface on planet Earth. Since such a population density would leave no ground for food production, it is self-evident that the exponential rises in food production and human population would be halted by one means or another, long before 2330 CE.

For many reasons the problems that lay ahead for the human race made little impact on mankind generally in the 1950s. One reason, and perhaps the dominant one, is that humans have only a very limited intellectual ability to concern themselves with the fortunes of future generations beyond their own children, and to conduct their affairs in ways that will benefit future generations as well as themselves and their own children. Mankind, it has been said, does little more than 'coo' into the cots of its grandchildren. That, presumably, is because our genetic make-up is supportive of personal survival, with ruthless short-term selfishness being crucial to the survival of the individual, and to the further evolution of the species. It is by those means that genotypic adaptation to environmental change occurs. The notion that our descendants, even as close as our own grandchildren, could face mass starvation and the agonies of the conflicts that the struggle for tribal survival would generate, and all because of our preoccupation with our own brief lifetimes is, for most of us, unthinkable, and therefore unimaginable.

The risks that mankind was taking, in presuming that advances in agricultural science could produce sustenance enough to support a burgeoning human population, were well understood by the scientifically- and socially-literate in the 1950s. Then, however, mankind was preoccupied with what was seen as a greater threat to its future than that of a failed equation of food supplies and populations. The nuclear age was upon us, and the imminence of international conflict that could result in mass extermination rendered concern about the eventual overpopulation of our planet almost academic. Furthermore, since the only alternative to nuclear deterrence would be the more traditional uses of armies, adequate manpower would, as Napoleon had observed, be crucial. The governments of the nations principally enmeshed in the East-West clash of ideologies saw good reasons to play down any need for population control. Religious leaders, likewise, knew that numbers mean strength, and thus urged upon their adherents their intellectually dubious theological reasons for opposing birth control. The curiosity of this stance lies is the absence of any theological objection to medical procedures which extend life beyond the point where, otherwise, death would have occurred. Apparently deities have no say in the occurrence of death, for surely otherwise the medical profession would also receive priestly denunciations for usurping the will of a deity.

These were the issues that vexed my mind during my post war mature-student days. Practically all my post-graduate years were spent in the service of Britain's Agricultural Research Council,[1] and not that of its Medical Research Council, as was my original intention. Because my subsequent preoccupations were with fundamental aspects of animal physiology, while the practical applications of physiology to animal husbandry were the tasks of others, I cannot claim to have made any direct contributions to the agricultural endeavour to equate food productions with populations needing to be fed. Nevertheless, this concern about the achievement of that equation has stayed with me for this last half-century, and this volume is an endeavour to encapsulate my thoughts before my time runs out.

---

[1] The UK Agricultural Research Council was disbanded in the 1980s when the Conservative government argued that since agriculture is an industry conducted for profit, the industry itself should pay for any research needed to improve productivity and profit. This was a classic failure to understand the difference between what agriculture is for, and how the industry is conducted. Much of the initiative was thereby passed to the chemical industry, the first duty of which is to shareholders, and not to how best to feed the world.

Chapter Two
MALTHUSIAN CONSIDERATIONS

In 1798 the Reverend Doctor Thomas Malthus (1766–1834) published the first edition of his thesis entitled *An Essay on the Principle of Population.* The principal point made by Malthus in this thesis was the ultimate ineffectiveness of charity as a means of reducing the sufferings of the paupers living at the least privileged end of the social spectrum. Alms for the desperately poor could, he argued, provide only a brief easement of their suffering. Since their numbers are checked by the high mortality amongst their progeny, any improvement in their welfare and that of their children would lower the incidence of infant mortality. That could be considered laudable, but with more of the children of paupers surviving into adulthood and sexual maturity, there would be more breeding pairs and hence eventually even more children to be kept alive by alms. The need for charity would increase from generation to generation until ultimately, the burden on society could become too great for it to bear. Then, with the charity exhausted, or even just no longer increasable, there would be the re-emergence of the sufferings of hunger, disease, and early deaths, on a far greater scale than there would have been had there been no charity in the first place.

The more that Malthus considered the particular consequences of giving alms to the destitute, the more he realised that what he had expounded about the relationship between the size of a population and its food supplies was not peculiar to the human species, but applied to nature generally. It is a feature of both plants and animals that they generate more progeny than is necessary to sustain a stable population, and more progeny than there would be food enough for all to survive, to mature, and in the fullness of time, to reproduce. Since, in nature, the food supply does not adapt to population sizes, population sizes must adapt to the prevailing food supply; and the natural way by which this is done is for there to be a high rate of premature mortality amongst the progeny.

We now know, being post Darwin, what Malthus could not then know: that this process of natural mass culling is essential for the survival and the continuing evolution of a species. Those best fitted to survive in any particular set of environmental circumstances are the ones that live long enough to procreate. Though Malthus was not concerned with the contribution of excessive reproduction to the feeding of other organisms further along the food chain, he could and did discern the inevitability of populations always being at the upper limit of what the food supply could support, and being held there by the early death of those individuals unable to acquire sufficient food to sustain themselves.

It follows from this biological circumstance, from which mankind is evidently not exempt, that any addition to the food supply will allow the population to rise, but only to that density at which the population is again controlled by the early mortality of those most undernourished. Thus giving of alms, or any other process by which food is distributed more equitably, can only delay the re-establishment of a status quo in which early death is the regulator. No matter how much the food supply can be increased in the hope and expectation that it will put an end to destitution, its effect can only be temporary. Ultimately the consequence will be that the incidence of dire hunger, and therefore of suffering is far greater than it would have been if the food supply had not been increased.

In pointing out that alms giving is a self-defeating remedy for extreme poverty, Malthus did not overtly advocate the withholding of alms to the destitute so that the magnitude of destitution could be contained, but that is what was widely inferred. His preferred means of escape from the 'poverty trap' was the exercise of reproductive restraint.

There is no evidence that Malthus was emotionally unaffected by the sufferings of the economically most deprived sections of the population of the England of his day. Having studied mathematics as well as theology at Cambridge, however, he was trained not only in the doctrines of orthodox Anglican Christian theology, but also to heed the evidence of his senses, and the products of his reasoning. The likelihood is that Malthus struggled with the conflict that many of us know, between what we wish we could believe to be true, and what the available evidence and our intellectual analysis compels us to believe is true. It is also likely that, as a clergyman, Malthus anticipated the reactions of his theological peers to the publication of this thesis – much as Charles Darwin, a century and a half later, was fearful of distressing his devout wife with what he felt compelled to say about the evolution of animal and human life.

The question whether Thomas Malthus's thesis was sensible and worthy of scholarly consideration was almost wholly obscured by the fierce opposition voiced loudly and widely by his peers who habitually preached brotherly love and charity towards all mankind more often than they practised it. To leave one's fellow human beings to endure the sufferings of extreme hunger because of the possibility that charity towards them would exacerbate the problem of the needy years hence was so clearly contrary to the Christian principles of compassion that it was said by Bonar (1924) that Malthus 'was the best abused man of his age', and he still tends to get a bad press.

This antagonism is exemplified by the reaction of Malthus's former tutor at Cambridge, William Frend, who challenged the Malthusian notion that the unhindered prime purpose of marriage could have the same disastrous consequences for mankind as those that result from the natural reproductive excesses of other members of the animal kingdom. He believed, as the majority of God-fearing persons at that time were instructed to believe, that mankind had been *separately and specially created in the likeness of the Christian God*; and thereby had an ability to reason which is denied to all other forms of life. At the same time, and quite inconsistently, Frend argued that any deliberate interference with human procreation would be a violation of divine will because each human child is brought into being not only as a consequence of the fertilisation of an ovum by a sperm, but also by the specific will of God. Mankind is, therefore, ethically bound to succour every one of God's human creations, however burdensome that duty might be. The problem with this even more contentious proposition than that of Malthus is that pregnancy can result from acts of loveless lust, including rape. The logic of this is that the Deity gives the nod of approval to all manner of unseemly human activities that result in pregnancy; and is knowingly indifferent to the painful consequences of both unwanted and excessive reproduction.

The inconsistency of Frend's assertion lies in his proposition that mankind alone has the God-given ability to reason, and that that peculiar faculty ensures mankind's immunity from the consequences of excessive breeding. It was Malthus and not Frend who was endeavouring to exercise the power of reason to address, and to limit the consequences of a tendency of mankind that is common to animals generally. Having considered the unpleasantness of the natural way of sustaining populations at the level which the food supply will support, Malthus argued not that we should desist from interfering with nature, and just allow the inadequately fed progeny of paupers to die in infancy, but that pregnancy should be restricted either by persuasion or by compulsion. In Malthus's time the only recognised means of avoiding pregnancy was by the exercise of 'moral restraint', by which he meant a voluntary embargo on copulation. It did, indeed, become understood that those needful of alms also needed to be denied the right to cohabit as man and wife, and this was the rationale behind the seemingly inhuman nineteenth-century practice of keeping spouses apart in Poor Law institutions.

Malthus had realised that, in the short term, the obvious defence against the consequences of a population in excess of the number that could be fed adequately, and thereby kept healthy, would be to seek ways to increase the food supply. At that time, with the industrial and agricultural revolution barely begun, and with the development of the 'new' lands overseas as the agricultural suppliers of Europe still largely unrealised, Malthus observed that while populations can increase with a geometric progression, food production could not possibly be made to increase faster than in arithmetic progression. While the first part of that statement is correct, it is now evident that the second part must be incorrect. If food availability had not also grown geometrically after Malthus's time, the human population of the world could not have increased geometrically. Needful of a more substantial stick with which to beat Malthus than that which theology provided, his critics have pounced on this one time-bound fault in Malthus's postulations. What he wrote, however, was true at the end of the eighteenth century. Historically, food production had increased only slowly, and more or less linearly with time; and in consequence the human population of the world had increased only slowly and more or less linearly with time. As anyone placing yeast cells in a vat of warm energy-rich fluid can attest, where the nutrient supply is not the restraining influence, population growth is indeed geometric. If, however, the food supply is continuously maintained, but increased at only a relatively restricted rate, then it is the extent of the food supply that determines the extent of the population growth.

There is nothing of a fixed law about the rate of growth of the food supply. It is a variable, depending on environmental circumstances. This unguarded statement on the limited rate of growth of the food supply by Malthus is often cited as a reason for ridiculing him, with the inference that that one overstatement negates the entire Malthusian thesis. It does not. Malthus was right to say that in favourable circumstances populations can grow exponentially, whereas increases in food production at anything like an exponential rate do not occur naturally. While it is easy to give reasons for disliking what Malthus felt compelled to say, to disprove him by intellectual effort has proved exceedingly difficult.

Malthus stated that 'as has been pointed out by many writers' populations are always kept down to that level for which there is sufficient subsistence, and added that his 'discussion of this interesting subject is activated solely by a love of truth, and not by any prejudice against any particular set of man or of opinion'. The same could not be said by Engels (1844) who based his rejection of the Malthusian population theory on grounds of prejudice rather than of reason. He described the build-up to Malthus's theory as 'sham philanthropy' and the theory as 'a blasphemy against nature and mankind which struck down all the beautiful phrases about love of neighbours and world citizenship'. Thus Engels, the 'material theologian', like Frend, the 'etherial theologian', preferred what it would be nice to believe, than what the latent ability to reason would cause one to believe. Engels, however, could not sustain his preference for his own brand of 'sham philanthropy' to the end, and in 1881 wrote in a letter, 'There is, of course, the abstract possibility that the number of people will become so great that limits will have to be set to their increase.'

There is now every reason to believe that this Malthusian proposition was, and is, basically correct. Humans, like other animals, will breed in excess of the number of progeny which can be fed into and through maturity; and the natural way by which populations are sustained at the supportable density is by the premature death of the excess progeny. Any increase in the food supply will result in an increase in the population, but unless there is a continually increasing food supply, there will be a return to the status quo in which early mortality will be controlling the population. Thus Malthus reasoned that the only way to contain the number of progeny to be fed without the agonies of the natural process of population control is for the birth rate to be controlled. At the end of the eighteenth century, however, faith was still a more powerful influence than was reason, so there is no difficulty in understanding why so many of Malthus's fellow clergymen reacted as adversely as they did. These numerous critics did not show that Malthus was misguided as a scholar, but only that his thesis offended the scruples of the society in which he lived.

Although it was Thomas Malthus who explicitly stated the unfortunate consequences of seeking to resolve the spectacle of hunger by the provision of alms to the poor, the basic reason for poverty and hunger had been pointed out already by Adam Smith some twenty years earlier in his text on economics, *The Wealth of Nations* (1776). Adam Smith stated that 'every species of animals naturally multiplies in proportion to the means of their subsistence, and no species can ever multiply beyond it'. It is evident that Adam Smith was in no doubt that human beings enjoy no exception to this biological generalisation; that they fully share this propensity to create more progeny than the food supply could sustain to maturity, and that many die in infancy when the food supply is inadequate. He pointed out, however, that with humans the consequential incidence of infant mortality is not uniformly distributed, but is highest amongst those most economically deprived. He wrote:

> In a civilised society it is only among the inferior ranks of people that the scantiness of subsistence can set limits to the further multiplication of the human species, and it can only do so in no other way than by destroying a great part of the children which their fruitful marriages produce.

Adam Smith thereby accepted that those with adequate access to the necessities of life will be the most successful breeders, while those that lack such support suffer the pains of hunger and the early demise of many of their children. In the 'civilised society' of which Adam Smith wrote, much of the hunger of the destitute was because others were hogging far more food than was needed for their health and happiness, leaving too little to be shared amongst the others. The implication of Adam Smith's consideration was that dire poverty in countries that were generally economically successful is the consequence of human greed, and that a more equitable distribution of essential commodities would relieve the situation. Alms for the poor can thus be considered as at least a progression towards a more equitable distribution. Malthus, it would seem, detected the fallacy of this remedy. Since populations tend to expand to the limit that their food supplies will support, and are then held at that level by the incidence of untimely deaths of the least well fed, even the most equitable distribution of the available food supply would afford only brief relief from hunger.

Malthus's first enunciation of the paradoxical and wholly unintended consequence of alms giving followed quite closely upon the publication of the *Principles of Morals and Legislation* (1789) by the constitutional lawyer, Jeremy Bentham, who was also concerned with finding a way to alleviate human suffering occasioned by extreme poverty. In that treatise, Bentham wrote 'The object of all legislation should be for the greatest happiness for the greatest number.'

The difference was that Bentham was an unrepentant and optimistic idealist who believed that an innate morality of mankind could outweigh the less magnanimous human tendencies; and that once mankind appreciated the ethical correctness of the equal distribution of the basic necessities of life there could, indeed, be that utopian society in which the greatest happiness for the greatest number is achieved. So while Malthus undoubtedly would have found the Benthamite aspiration as laudable as Adam Smith's supposed remedy, he saw the fallacy of both these ideals. The human genetic inheritances of an insatiable urge to reproduce, coupled to the endeavour of each individual to obtain and protect the best for his or her self at anyone else's cost, means that whatever is done to resolve hunger, there will always be the survival of only as many mouths to feed as there is food to put into them. The urge for self-preservation will ensure that the food supply will not be equally distributed, and for so long as the propensity to reproduce is unrestrained, happiness for all will remain an unattainable ideal. The giving of alms to the destitute to facilitate their well-being will never achieve more than a brief relief, and will eventually exacerbate the problem.

Even Adam Smith's discernment that more mouths to feed than there is food for always means the miseries of hunger, disease and early death for the losers in the scramble for enough to eat, and Thomas Malthus's realisation that nothing else than population control could protect mankind from those afflictions, were rediscoveries of an ancient wisdom. As a student more than fifty years ago, I attended a lecture by Dr Marie Stopes, who early in the twentieth century had been an active protagonist of birth control in order to alleviate the human suffering that can attend upon unwanted and unaffordable pregnancies. She told us that several pre-Christian societies are known to have exercised birth control, or the control of survival after birth. Marie Stopes told her audience that both ancient Egyptian and ancient Chinese communities had recognised the need to restrict population as a defence against unnecessary suffering when human numbers were more than could be supported, as occurred periodically due to crop failures. To that end the Egyptians used intravaginal sponges soaked in vinegar as a spermicide, while the Chinese used down feathers soaked in oil as a sperm barrier. In other societies, particularly perhaps, those of nomadic herdsmen in the Euro-Asian regions, populations were prevented from outgrowing the productivity of their pastures by post-natal infanticide. In Malthus's time these earlier examples of population control were unknown, and Malthus saw no means of controlling birth other than by voluntary or enforced abstinence from sexual unity.

Why has Thomas Malthus been so harshly considered and so persistently misinterpreted? Could it be that what Adam Smith and Thomas Malthus had to say on the matter of populations and their food supplies was considered too correct and too unpalatable for popular consumption? Or was it that, like Galileo Galilei before him, his reasoning conflicted with the theological dogmas of his day? I am more suspicious of the motives of the decriers of Malthus, than those of Malthus himself.

Many, for theological or ideological reasons, do not want to admit to the fundamental correctness of the Malthusian analysis, and lay undue emphasis on that one understandable overstatement by Malthus as reason enough to rubbish him. The overstatement was Malthus's assertion that while populations could grow geometrically if there was food enough to permit it, the rate of increase in food production was only ever arithmetic. The mathematical expression implied that food never could increase other than slowly and linearly, and we now know that that is not true. It should be noted, however, that at no time in the two millennia preceding the eighteenth century had food production increased other than slowly and fairly linearly. Nearly 200 years on, the journalist A Marr (1998) wrote:

> We all know Malthus got it wrong. Malthus's explanation of the coming poverty, environmental decay and social collapse… has gone down as one of history's great failed predictions – not just wrong but hilariously wrong.

I wish that were true, but Marr viewed the issue retrospectively and not prospectively. There is yet time to discover that Malthus got it right. Those who search the world beyond their comfortable armchairs will find evidence enough today of poverty, environmental decay and social collapse. Marr's contribution was not hilariously wrong, but just sadly and blindly wrong.

Chapter Three
HUMAN POPULATIONS

Introduction

For long the ignorance of mankind about its origins allowed it the vanity of believing itself to have been especially created and protected, and therefore to be immune from the harsh terms and conditions of animal life generally. However, well before Charles Darwin's seminal studies, *The Origin of Species* (1859) and *The Descent of Man* (1871), which provided a quite different measure of the status of Homo sapiens, it was already evident from Adam Smith's *The Wealth of Nations* (1776) and Thomas Malthus's *Essay on the Principle of Population* (1796) that the reproductive propensity of Homo sapiens is essentially that of animals generally, as indeed Lucretius had discerned some 2,000 years earlier. In the absence of any restraint, human beings reproduce to a greater extent than is necessary to sustain the numerical stability of a population. In consequence, human populations always tend to increase to the limits that their food supplies will allow. They can seldom increase to far beyond that limit, and then only briefly. When that level is reached populations are then held in check by the premature death of those obtaining insufficient food to sustain life. It is in this context that the history and the prognostication of human populations must be considered.

This excessive reproduction occurs in plants as well as in animals. Indeed without this excessive fruiting of plants, animals would not exist, for it is the excessive seed production of cereal plants that provides much of the food for humans and their herbivorous domesticated animals. The brewing industry provides a salutary example of the relationship between food supplies and populations. Brewing not only depends on surplus plant seeds as the principal energy source, but also upon the unrestrained multiplication of the yeast cells when the food supply is plentiful and the environment is rendered optimal. The multiplication of the yeast cells continues only for so long as the nutrient supply lasts out and the environmental conditions are tolerable. Eventually the nutrients become exhausted and/or the environment becomes toxically polluted by the alcoholic end-products of yeast cell metabolism. A population crash is then bound to occur.

A similar story could be told of almost any other organism when, for a time, the supply of nutrients is unlimited, but eventually becomes inadequate. There is no reason or evidence that allows the presumption that the human species is not embarked on a similar course, with its numbers increasing as the food supply is progressively increased. There is now reason to be concerned as to whether the food supplies needed for the present inflated world population can be sustained, and whether, like the yeast cells in the brewer's vat, we are toxically polluting the environment with our own waste products, to our increasing detriment. If either of these looming dangers becomes large enough, a human population crash could become inevitable. In this chapter the topic under consideration is the growth of human populations. In the next chapter the growth of human food supplies, and their sustainability, will be examined. Attention will then turn to aspects of the pollution of the environment resulting from human activities on such expanding scales.

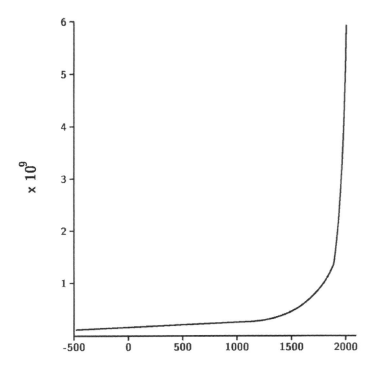

FIG. 3.1   THE CHANGE IN THE ESTIMATED HUMAN POPULATION OF THE WORLD DURING THE LAST 2,500 YEARS TO THE END OF THE TWENTIETH CENTURY (BASED ON MCEVEDY AND JONES, 1978).

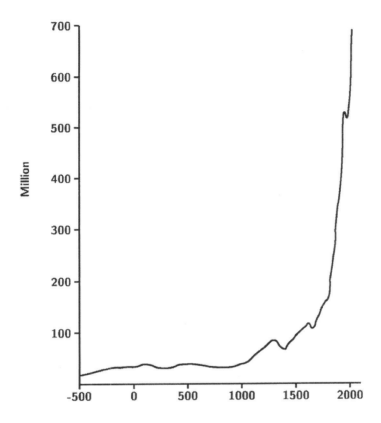

FIG. 3.2   THE CHANGE IN EUROPEAN HUMAN POPULATION BETWEEN 500 BCE AND 2000 CE (BASED ON A FIGURE BY MCEVEDY AND JONES, 1978)

Date	World Population (million)	Time taken to double (years)
400 BCE	100	
600 CE	200	1,000
1430	400	830
1775	800	240
1900	1,600	125
1970	3,200	70
2010?	6,400	40

TABLE 3.1   THE TIMES TAKEN FOR THE HUMAN POPULATION OF THE WORLD TO DOUBLE SINCE 400 BCE

Human Populations Historically

A plot of the estimated world population over the last 2,400 years (Fig. 3.1), taken from the *Atlas of World Population* collated by McEvedy and Jones (1978), indicates that human numbers rose only slowly and fairly linearly, from about 100 million in 400 BCE to about 425 million in 1600 CE. This approximately fourfold increase means that the population doubled only twice in 2,000 years. This contrasts with the 40 years it took for the world population to double from 3,000 million to 6,000 million between 1960 and 1999. The dramatic and progressive shortening of the time taken for the world population to double in the course of the last two to three centuries (Table 3.1) cannot be reasonably or substantially attributed to any change in circumstances other than an equally dramatic and progressive increase in the availability of food.

Figure 3.2, also taken from McEvedy and Jones (1978), shows that a marked change in the rate of increase in human populations occurred in Europe in the course of the seventeenth century. It then continued to grow at a increasing rate until almost the end of the twentieth century. The speeding up of the rate of increase in the populations of other regions, China for example, followed soon after. Elsewhere, such as Canada, a marked changed in the rate of population did not occur until the nineteenth century.

When these population changes are pooled as changes in the human population of the world (Fig. 3.1) the pattern is not unlike that of Europe, except that the onset of the increase in population is not evident on that scale until towards the end of the eighteenth century. Fluctuations in regional population curves occurred both before and after the dramatic changes in the rates of increase. Brief falls in populations relate to local circumstances such as famines, epidemics or war; but only the largest of these are evident on plots of the changes in world population.

Effects of Massive Mortality

The quite profound dip in the plot of the population of Europe between 1300 and 1500 (Fig. 3.2) was caused by the bubonic plague which, during the fourteenth century, resulted in the death of about 25% of the European population, which was some 80 million when the plague struck. By the end of the fifteenth century, however, the population was back to what it was before the plague. There must have been some reduction in food production during the time of the plague, but it would seem that for a while after the plague had passed there was ample food for the depleted population. This improved the prospects of survival, especially of infants, and consequently it took less than one hundred years for the European population to recover. Recovery from the less dramatic population depression in the first half of the seventeenth century, brought about by the heavy mortality during the Thirty Years' War between Catholics and Protestants (1618–1649) also took only fifty years. Likewise, the appalling carnage in Europe in the course of the first half of the twentieth century, which was occasioned by the two World Wars, systematic acts of genocide and the influenza epidemic after the first Word War, resulted in only the briefest downward blip in the upward progress of the population curve.

These, and many other incidents of rapid recovery from a precipitous population decline occasioned by circumstances other than persistent famine, are consistent with the food supply being the determinant of population size. Since procreativity is at most

FIG. 3.3   A COMPARISON OF THE REGIONS OF THE WORLD (SHOWN IN SOLID
BLACK) WHERE THE CHILDREN PER WOMAN WAS 4.5 OR MORE IN THE
PERIOD 1970–1975 (A), AND IN THE PERIOD 2000–2005 (B).
(EXTRACTED FROM THE GRAPHIC REPRESENTATION OF THE
WORLDWIDE DISTRIBUTION OF FERTILITY RATES BY CINCOTTA,
ENGELMAN AND ANASTASION, 2003.)

times greater than survival possibility, when food become readily available after a population crash, more infants can survive and mature than would otherwise have been possible. The population will then rise quite quickly until the limitation of the food supply again prohibits further expansion.

Because of the inborn capacity to breed in excess of replacement needs there will always be more infants needing to be fed than the food supply can support into maturity. Thus for so long as the birth rate is uncontrolled, it is inevitable that a proportion of the newborn infants will die of starvation, or of disease against which a starving child has little defence. It is largely by this natural process of culling that the population is determined by the food supply. This means, of course, that massive losses of life by epidemic diseases, wars and genocide demonstrate that death – by whatever cause, and on whatever scale – will have little, if any, long-term influence on the size of populations when there is no substantial change in the availability of food. Although such occurrences have only brief effects on populations, as is evident from Fig. 3.2, they have permanent effects on the ethnic and genetic composition of subsequent populations. That, however, is another matter.

Frank Ryan in *Tuberculosis: The Greatest Story Never Told* (1992) states that in the course of the nineteenth and twentieth centuries 1,000 million people, worldwide, died of tuberculosis, which amounts to an average annual death rate of some 5 million. It has also been estimated that before there was any way to combat malaria, which was not until halfway through the twentieth century, one in four deaths worldwide were the result of malaria. With the world population at 2,500 million in 1950, and assuming that the average life expectancy worldwide was then fifty years, the total death rate would have been of the order of 40 million per year. Each year as many as 10 million of these deaths could have been caused by malaria, while the combined annual deaths from tuberculosis and malaria were of the order of 15 million per year, or more than a third of all deaths.

Each individual death is, for families and friends, a tragic loss of life. In terms of population statistics, however, it is a rapidly replaced loss, for each withdrawal from the food market allows the survival of another 'customer'. Consequently, if the food supply is undiminished, no matter what the death rate is, and whether it is at a continuous rate, as it was with tuberculosis, or a dramatic loss as in a major war or act of genocide, the effect on the population is not for long. The differences between population control by hunger, microbial diseases or warfare are thus qualitative and not quantitative. Numerically the population will recover rapidly, but there will be qualitative changes because some germ lines will have been halted, while others will have continued.

With disease and human belligerency being major causes of truncated lifetimes besides that of hunger per se, there is the survival, and then the procreation, of those best fitted to survive in the prevailing adverse circumstances. Some selection will be based on resistance to infections, and some determined by success at war, or at avoiding war. With escape from either or both of these hazards, the selection will then be of those best suited to other prevailing circumstances, a major one being the ability to compete successfully for enough food for oneself and one's progeny. That will often lead to belligerency, for in drastic circumstances food needs to be fought for.

Thus I am here at the present time because my ancestors were survivors through successive generations from the dawn of life right to my parents. During World War I, my father, just old enough to be sent to Flanders, was instead sent to India to replace regular soldiers destined for the trenches in Europe, and so he survived to breed, while his brother died in Flanders without issue. My son is here, perhaps, because, in World War II the British Army dispensed with my services early in the conflict. My brother was killed without issue. My wife could tell a similar story, and every one of us, aware of his or her family tree, could cite their own particular pathway of survival. The death of my father's brother left a scar in my father's psyche, and my brother's early death has left a scar in mine. Both deaths were deeply felt personal losses, but neither death reduced the total human population for long. In each instance, there was then food enough for someone else to stay alive. Thus although over the last 200 years tuberculosis has claimed a thousand million lives, and each loss was a personal loss to a family; and although each death will have affected the genetic composition of those now living, the horrendous struggle between Homo sapiens and *Mycobacterium tuberculosis* has had no influence upon the magnitude of the present world population. The same goes for every other loss of life great or small, and whether natural or inflicted by mankind upon itself.

Birth, then, can be likened to an application for a food ration book. If the food supply is unchanging, the ration books will always be fully distributed. Whether or not a new arrival gets one depends upon someone else, somewhere else in the world, having yielded up theirs for re-allocation. If the food supply can be increased, that is tantamount to the issue of additional ration books. That allows the population to rise until they have all been issued. From then on, unless food production continues to rise, each new entrant into the mass of humanity will depend upon a death to occur for a ration book to become available. Obviously there would be fewer disappointed applicants for a food ration if the number of applicants could be kept more or less in balance with the death rate and/or any change in the food supply. In the absence of such control, there is always a proportion of newly born applicants who will be unsuccessful in their bid, and will consequently die prematurely.

It is, however, not so simple an equation. At the present time about half the world gets along very well on two ration books per person, while most of the other half have to share their ration books, each individual getting some food, but not enough to keep fit. Generally speaking you can tell the one category from the other by the mean waist measurements of the members of each category.

Partly because of the unequal distribution of the world's food production, partly because of periods of drought and famine, and partly because the birth rate is uncontrolled, there has probably never been a time when every newly born child has stood a fair chance of surviving to maturing, and of then being adequately fed throughout its adult life. Depending upon one's definition of hunger – to what extent it is life-threatening, and whether it is seasonal or continuous – it has been variously estimated that anything from 20% to 40% of the human population of the world are suffering some degree of hunger today. It is likely that the percentage has not changed greatly during the last 2,000 years at least. If that is so, then the quantity of suffering has increased as the population has increased. When, 2,000 years ago, the estimated world population was less than 200 million, the 20% likely to have been painfully underfed amounted to a mere 40 million persons. At 1000 CE, when the world population was still only about 300 million most likely there would have been 60 million underfed. At 2000 CE, when the world population has reached 6,000 million, 20% in a state of hunger amounted to some 1,200 million persons. The moral of this is that if population growth is unrestrained, while food production is being progressively increased, the magnitude of the hunger in the world is also increasing progressively. The number of hungry people in the world today equals the entire population of the world only 150 years ago.

With our particular ability to know something of our history, and to consider where, as a species and as sharing tenants of planet Earth, we are heading, we are capable – if we so choose – of contemplating future human generations and what their inheritance from us is likely to be. It is in the ability to contemplate the future, and to provide for it, that we differ from other animals. Whatever the strictly biological significance of unmoderated procreation and the ruthless processes of selection that must follow from it, we have the latent ability to consider how best to serve mankind in perpetuity, and not just how best to serve ourselves during our own brief lifetimes. For that we must strive to sustain and strengthen the integrity of that thin veneer of humanity by which we seek to subdue our animal inheritances, and ensure, to the best of our ability, that we leave the world in a fit state for our successors.

To do that we must return to this issue of population and food supplies. For so long as reproduction is uncontrolled there will always be more newly arrived mouths to feed than food to satisfy them all, so there will always be a substantial incident of infantile deaths resulting from malnutrition. There will always be a substantial proportion of humanity that is hungry to some degree periodically or permanently, and is anxious to improve its lot. There will always be the adequately fed communities anxious to preserve their lifestyles and food supplies for their members and their families. There will always be, while there is this division of fortunes, a cause for conflict, with one party seeking to gain food, and the other party seeking to retain it. And conflicts based on food will often require the extermination of the vanquished, for land acquired in battle is most valuable when there is vacant possession.

The only way to break these patterns of behaviour, which are based upon the struggle for individual survival, and which are characteristic of animals generally, is to assert our humanity, and ensure by the most humane of means that populations are not allowed to outreach their food supplies; that is by birth control.

The Future

The rate of increase in world population seems now to have levelled out with an annual rate of increase of about 90 million, which is approximately a quarter of a million more mouths to feed with every passing day. This increase means that the birth rate is in excess of the death rate by that amount, partly because progressively more mating couples tends to result in progressively more births, and partly because of the reduction in the death rate due to improved health and increased longevity. This sustained rise in population can occur, however, only because there is a sufficiently large increase in the world food supply to feed an additional 90 million persons each year. This rate of increase in the human population, which has been geometric during the last two or three centuries, seems now to be arithmetic, or linear. If this linear progression is sustained the world population will have doubled to 12,000 million before the end of the twenty-first century. That could only occur, of course, if the world food supply can be doubled in the course of the present century.

The demographic forecast is that the rate of increase in the world population will not be sustained, but will progressively decline such that the population of the world will level out at around 9,000 million in fifty years' time. Such statements are treated by some as a comforting indication that fears of gross overpopulation are unwarranted, and that no drastic measures to curb population need be taken. Generally speaking, however, the demographers do not provide details of the supposed circumstances and occurrences that will account for the eventual stabilisation of the human population.

Whatever the computed trends may show, whether or not the population will rise to 9,000 million and will then stabilise at that level will depend, more than anything else, upon the level of food production and the extent to which it is equitably distributed. As is discussed in Chapter Four, there are indications of an increasing frailty of some of the conditions and practices upon which intensified agricultural production now depends. Even if the benefits of genetically modified crops are as anticipated and provide the means by which human nutritional needs can be satisfied, there is no certainty that the further demands upon agricultural land needed to feed increasing populations will be sustainable throughout the present century and beyond. Perhaps supplies of water for irrigation will be the first to collapse; perhaps it will not be possible to continue to apply high levels of inorganic minerals to the soil without polluting the water we drink. What is certain is that the extant 6,000 million Homo sapiens is a grossly unnatural population density, which is already demanding too much from the soil and causing too much pollution of the environment. We are already courting the danger of a collapse of food supplies and/or of creating such levels of environmental pollution that a population crash will be the result.

Any rise in population inevitably means an increase in the number of breeding pairs, and therefore in the fullness of time to an increase in the numbers of birth. So what do the demographers suppose will stabilise the world population at 9,000 million? There would seem to be only two possibilities. The one is that of nature, which is by an increase in deaths resulting from hunger, and particularly in infancy, will keep the population densities at whatever levels the prevailing food supply will support. The other way, which only our own species can resort to, is to keep the birth rate down voluntarily.

Inevitably, theological or other doctrines that seek to place an embargo on voluntary birth control are, consciously or not, opting for the natural process of population control and all the suffering that that must cause. This can be seen to be operating in some South American communities where voluntary birth control is strongly discouraged. In contrast, where there is that degree of education that lays emphasis upon the ability to think for oneself, there is the increasing tendency of mated pairs to opt for small families of only two or three children. One factor in such decisions is the reduction in infant mortality resulting from improvements in pre- and post-natal care. There is less need then for parents to anticipate premature deaths as in former times.

Other factors are cultural and economic. Parents want to give their children the best opportunity to succeed in a competitive environment. They realise that it is better to provide suitable educational opportunities and social advantages for each child in a small family, than to struggle to provide such opportunities for every child in a large family. Thus it is in those societies where potential opportunities for one's children are greatest and education is least doctrinaire, that population densities are tending to stabilise without the indignities and sufferings of natural population control. In these communities the fear of hunger is not a major consideration since strong economies allow the purchase of food from elsewhere in the world, largely regardless of what the consequences might be to those who export the food. Even, however, in societies still struggling to achieve the benefits enjoyed by the economically most privileged ones, and where there is fear of hunger, there is increasing evidence of voluntary birth control. Improvements in pre- and post-natal care, combined with a greater opportunity for the female partner to influence the decision of how many children a couple will have, is also reducing the size of families, and the rates of population growth.

Population control by means of pregnancy control is now a discussible subject in many of the more enlightened societies, and the means of effecting it are readily available, but not always at affordable prices. Some governments have therefore recognised the social and economic benefit of subsidising the distribution of contraceptive devices. In some countries in which populations are rising, and where there is a fear of what the consequences could be, penalties are imposed on parents that exceed a stipulated family size. Whether, however, family limitation is by individual decision or by governmental pressure, the slowing down and perhaps the ultimate elimination of population increases will provide the best hope of avoiding the pending disaster of massive famine or massive environmental pollution.

With the objective of enabling political and military leaders to anticipate which regions, economies and social structures are most likely to lead to regional unrest or inter-regional conflicts, Cincotta, Engelman and Anastasion (2003) have studied the extent to which demographic analyses can be used to predict the stability or instability of countries or regions. They have found that populations with high birth and death rates are more likely to suffer civil disturbances than those with lower birth and death rates; and that on average, a decline in the annual birth rate by 5 births per thousand of the population, correlates with a 5% reduction in civil conflicts. They also found a distinct relationship between the mean age of a community and the likelihood of conflict. A high proportion of young adults of 15–29 years of age – described as a 'youth bulge' – is conducive to social unrest, especially in urban environments. The relationship between populations and their social stabilities is surely affected by many variables. Inadequate supplies of food and water are obvious reasons for discord both within communities and between communities. An imbalance of the ratio of the sexes can also be another cause of strife, and intra-territorial and inter-territorial ethnic and religious differences tend to lower the flashpoint of aggression, whether or not such differences are the a prime causes of antagonisms.

Two findings by Cincotta et alii are of particular interest and importance. One is the evidence of a strong correlation between the use of contraceptives and the number of births per woman. This is almost linear, with births per woman falling from an average of about 6 to less than 2 as the use of methods of contraception increases. The demographic transition that results from the widespread use of contraceptives lowers the likelihood of conflict. This could be because there is then less hunger and other social deprivations that high population densities give rise to. The other point of interest is the comparison of the worldwide distribution of human fertility in 1970–1975 with that anticipated for 2000–2005. The regions where the average number of births per woman is 4.5 or now markedly smaller than they were twenty-five years ago. Fig. 3.3 is an extraction from one by Cincotta et alii to show the global regions where the mean number of children per woman was 5 or more in the periods 1970–1975 and 2000–2005. Only in Africa, the Middle East and the Indian subcontinent are there still these large numbers of births per woman generally. Whereas poverty and social deprivation is part of the cause, authoritarian religions must also carry the burden of responsibility for the consequential suffering. The reductions in family sizes elsewhere could relate to less acceptance of priestly guidance, the wider availability and use of birth-control techniques, and changes in social attitudes which allow women a greater control over the frequency of pregnancy could be a significant underlying factor.

Indeed, it is at least arguable that the universal sexual franchisement of women could be the most effective way of curbing the expansion in the human population of the world. The strongest opposition to moves away from male domination in sexual matters, and the acceptance of birth control as a matter of humanity in the short term, and necessity in the long term, is by authoritarian theologies. As the world population increases, so do the numbers of hungry humans and premature deaths. It is thus becoming increasingly clear that those who are opposed to birth control are not, as they purport to be, true champions of the 'right to life' but, to the contrary, are the unwitting advocates of ever more miserable lives and early deaths.

The adverse effect of halting the rise in human populations is that for a while the mean age of populations will rise. There would then be more unproductive elderly persons requiring economic support than workers generating funds for the support of the elderly. This adverse consequence of birth control is exacerbated by the endeavours of the medical profession to progressively increase life expectancy. These handicaps cannot be minimised, and need to be planned for. One solution could be to encourage people to stay working for as long as they are able and willing to do so.

If, by one means or another, the world population does stabilise at 9,000 million, that equilibrium state will be because the rates of births and deaths are in balance. If the worldwide average duration of a lifetime is 60 years, one person in sixty, that is 150 million persons, would be dying each year, and thereby creating the opportunity for 150 million neonates to survive and mature. A popular perception is that all neonate lives could be saved from early extinction, and that mature lives could be progressively extended to whatever extent the medical sciences can make possible, with no adverse consequences to blight the promise. If we suppose that when the world population is 9 billion, the medical profession then succeeds in extending the average duration of a lifetime worldwide to, say, 70 years, the immediate effect would be to reduce the annual death rate from 150 million to 128.5 million. If the medical benefits responsible for this were to be effected worldwide, and if there was no possibility of a further increase in world's food supplies, the population could then remain unchanged only if the birth rate and/or the postnatal survival rate is reduced to the same extent. Such a reduction in the birth rate could occur only by a deliberate change in the human reproductive behaviour pattern. Without it the inevitable and natural population adjustment would be by an increase in infant mortality.

It might be supposed that an increase in food supply, if possible, would prevent this, and render birth control unnecessary. Such relief, however, would be short-lived, for this would pave the way for a further rise in population, until the limitation of the food supply was again the principal population determinant. Increases in the food supply can never catch up with the increase in birth rate and the demand for food. No matter how successful we are in increasing food production, without population control there will continue to be hunger and hunger-induced mortality, particularly amongst infants. The continuing effort to equate world food production and world population is thus an upward spiral that obviously could not continue indefinitely as if it were a double helix of infinite length. The time would surely come when food production could be increased no further, or might even fall slowly or precipitously. This would cause a slow or a rapid population crash as the death rate soars above the birth rate, and populations decline numerically.

Thus, as Boulding (1959) had pointed out, without birth control equilibrium between resources and population is maintainable only by the misery of starvation and premature death, or by the human vice of genocide, as individuals, families or tribes seek to supply their own needs at any other individual's, family's or tribe's expense. In principle, at least, the issue is quite simple. Either we keep our number at or below that which the food supply can sustain, or we can refuse to do so, and suffer the same process of natural population control that animals generally must suffer.

Claims that there is some other way by which populations can be kept within the limit of sustainability, or that Homo sapiens enjoys some special dispensation which will protect it from the inevitable agonies that excessive reproduction must cause, are unsupported by either historical or contemporary evidence. Such beliefs may bring comfort to some, the lucky well-fed ones, but not to those who are hungry. It should now be evident, however, that these are doctrines of selfish complacency which, when widely adopted, contribute to a great deal of avoidable human suffering. It behoves mankind, if it has the corporate sense to do so, to take whatever steps are necessary to ensure that the world population is not allowed to increase to beyond that number which can be supported by sustainable food supplies. Already there are those who doubt whether, even with the promises of a GM-based boost to world food supplies, it will be possible to achieve and sustain sufficient food production to support the present human population of 6,000 million indefinitely. Still less can there be any certainty that a population of 9,000 million will be supportable well into the future.

Irrespective of whether the world food supply can be increased by some 50% within the next fifty years, and sustained at that level thereafter, the social implications of the predicted increase in the mass of humanity deserves serious consideration. Urban growth is now outstripping rural growth by 3:1, and it seems likely that within the next fifty years half the world's population will live in urban communities. Those who already reside in the great conurbations, and have to live, commute and work in such stifling and unnatural environments, cannot relish the prospects of living in cities that are half as big again as they are now, or of there being many more cities than there are now. There is already little ground for hope that all the extant 6,000 millions human beings could be afforded anything approaching the fully and universally shared quality of life that Jeremy Bentham yearned for. There can be even less hope that with 9,000 million concurrent lives on Earth, everyone's life could be enjoyed and fulfilled.

From this discussion on population it is evident that except when human activity interferes with the progression, changes in populations almost always follow changes in the food supply. Cultural factors, and other circumstances and events, however, can over-ride this direct relationship. As is discussed later, in some parts of the world food production has long been much greater than regional needs, yet in contrast to the rapid recoveries of populations that have occurred after devastations by diseases or wars, populations of regions such as those of North America and Australasia remain well below the maxima that could be supported by indigenous food supplies. Amongst the possible explanations for this is the rapidity and the extent of the increases in food production once agriculture got underway in these 'new-found lands', and which was largely in response to the export opportunities. The exportation of excess agricultural produce remains an important part of the economies of those regions, and so provides an incentive to restrict population growth. This motivation is compounded by the seductive cultural benefits of high living standards and health care, which allow more interests and objectives in life than just raising the next generation. Hence the voluntary suppression of the birth rate. In other countries where food production may not be greatly in excess of needs, industrial growth and the exportation of manufactured goods provides the economic ability to import all the additional food supplies that are needed, and to support high health and living standards. In such emerging countries there may not be the growth in populations that these conditions could allow, and this is possibly because a high standard of living that can be best enjoyed by smaller families, and because of the reduced need to anticipate the premature deaths of some of their progeny. Thus in these regions also, populations remain below the feedable maximum.

Elsewhere, however, and particularly where the restraining influences of economic stability and heightened living standards are absent, birth rates are much higher, and populations tend to be at the limit of supportability, with the premature deaths of the excess progeny being the natural process by which population growth is held in check. In this circumstance any reduction in the food supply, such as occurs when there is a food crop failure, will have the immediate effect of dramatically increasing the extent of hunger, and of premature deaths. Thus, as I am writing this, Bob Geldof, who raised funds through 'Band-Aid' twenty years ago to alleviate the misery and starvation of children in drought- and famine-stricken regions of Africa, now finds that his rescue operation needs to be repeated. Those children saved by Geldof's first effort are now of reproductive age, so there are more mated couples than there would otherwise be. Without birth rate restraint, population control has to be by the premature deaths of 'excess' progeny.

International aid organisations such as UNICEF and the 'Save the Children Fund' must surely know that the crises to which they respond are bound to recur, unless steps are taken to keep birth rates at or below those which will allow all the progeny to survive and mature. Only if birth rates are held down will there be a sufficient differential between populations and their food supplies to protect against periodic harvest failures. The most likely reason for this lack of the necessary advocacy of birth control to avert further periods of severe malnutrition is a deference towards those that teach, or have been taught to believe, that deliberate birth control is sinful. This silence was rationalised when a director of one of the charitable aid organisations was questioned. The reply was that such action is unwarranted, because as the famine-stricken countries develop their economies, their births will fall to within the feedable levels, as has occurred in 'developed' countries. Even if that does occur eventually, it will not be soon, and in the meanwhile the agonies of underfed children will persist. There are, it must be said, concurrent efforts to promote 'self-help' by assisted improvements in agricultural practices to increase food production. That, however, without birth control, is really no solution to the dilemma. It adds another twist to the spiralling interaction between food production and population, which cannot continue for ever. If, at any time (which means every time), the upward spiralling of food production and population is halted because the continuous expansion of agricultural productivity cannot be sustained, the natural population check of starvation and premature death must come into play.

To ignore this scenario, for whatever reason, is to wilfully tolerate the continuation of this painful means of keeping population and food supplies in balance. To suppose that a short pain-ridden life, being the will of a deity, is a better thing by far than no life at all, is surely, for the unindoctrinated humanist, beyond comprehension.

The worldwide human population, then, divides – though not sharply – between those with access to more food than is needed for their survival, and who stay that way by checking the rate of reproduction, and those with insufficient food for the survival of all new-arrivals, and with premature death as the means by which population growth is checked. With the persistence of this great divide between plenty and insufficient, it is evident that considered worldwide, the human population is being fixed by the extent of the food supply, with premature mortality being most prevalent amongst the less privileged sectors of humanity. This latter scenario is that of nature generally: the strong, who are the adequately fed, survive. The weak, who are the chronically underfed, do not.

The universality of this aspect of 'the survival of the fittest' throughout evolutionary history right through to the emergence of Homo sapiens, means that the instinct to get what one needs by whatever means it is within one's capacity to effect, has been continuously sustained and reinforced, and is strongly with us still. One does not have to be a student of sociology to note the continuous expression of this genetic inheritance.

A more equitable distribution of the world's food supplies is the dream of idealists. If only it could be effected it would allow the population of the world to rise to a new maximum achievable level. Without birth control, however, that would not eliminate hunger. At that new level, the population would again be determined by the food supply, with an even greater degree and spread of premature deaths than previously acting as the effector of population limitation.

For all the presumed intellectual superiority of the human species, it is not, generally speaking, adept at objective thought on matters of human relationships, which is wholly unconditioned by the dictates of animal instincts. Thus even if the need for reproductive limitations were to be generally accepted as necessary for long-term human welfare, it would be set aside when nature directed otherwise. This would be much as is a yearning for peace that is soon overridden when personal survival requires belligerency.

Preliminary indications are that the majority of women in both privileged and deprived societies will elect to have only 2–3 children if given the choice. Thus if the notion of sexual equality, which is now increasingly accepted in the more cultured societies, included joint decision over child-bearing, that might contribute substantially to the reduction in birth rate needed to lower the risk of a disastrous human population crash. The woman's preference for a small family need not now stifle the male libido, and thereby weaken the partnership, for mating pairs can select the means by which they effect family limitation.

Chapter Four

AGRICULTURE AND FOOD SUPPLIES

Introduction

It is now manifestly evident that in natural circumstances the extent of the availability of food is the principal determinant of population size. In the exceptional case of Homo sapiens, there are social and economic forces that distort this direct relationship between food supplies and populations. Even where food is plentiful, these social and economic considerations may keep the local population below the maximum number that could be fed, but more generally it is the availability of food that determines population sizes. This being so, it follows that progressive increases in human populations, considered over periods of centuries rather than decades, must be largely, if not entirely, the consequence of progressive increases in the food availability.

Food as a Vital Fuel

The French chemist Lavoisier (1743–1794) wrote, '*La vie est donc une combustion*' – Life is then a fire – when he realised that the dependency of animal life upon an adequate food supply is, in its basic chemistry, essentially the same as the dependency of a fire or any fire-driven machine, upon oxygen and a supply of fuel. As with all processes of burning, whether in an open fire or in any mechanical device that does work on the external environment, such as the internal combustion engine of a motor vehicle, an adequate fuel supply is essential. Fuel is always a complex chemical structure which, when catabolised (=broken down) into simpler molecular structures of less energy content, releases energy, which converts to heat immediately, or can be used directly to do work.

A fundamental particularity of the animal kingdom is that, unlike the plants, animals cannot capture solar energy and convert it into the chemical energy of the complex biochemical molecules of its own substance. For the energy needed for the building and maintenance of itself, and for the performance of work, an animal must rely, directly or indirectly, on the energy-rich molecules synthesised by plants. Once constructed and operational, the animal body is not just comparable with an internal combustion machine, but is one. A difference between an animal and most man-built machines, however, is that the 'engine' of an animal has to be kept idling, and therefore burning fuel, when it is otherwise totally inactive. It is, therefore, constantly using up fuel and this needs to be replenished from time to time whether or not it is being used to do external work. As with any other 'machine' the rate of fuel consumption, and the need for its replenishment, varies with its own size as well as its mechanical efficiency and the extent to which external work is being done. If, for any reason, the idling of the animal internal combustion system ceases, it cannot then be restarted, and the whole structure of the machine begins to disintegrate.

This essential similarity of engineered and organismic internal combustion processes clarifies the relationship between food supplies and populations. So long as the fuel supply for fuel-burning internal combustion engines is plentiful, as many units can be operational as are being manufactured and commissioned, and maintenance engineers can keep in good working order. Obviously, however, there can never be more machines in operation than can be kept supplied with fuel. When the fuel supply is virtually unlimited, there need be no limit to the production and to the operation of all the machines that are being produced. When, however, fuel is in short supply, the number of machines that can be kept in operation is limited accordingly. Unless production is then cut back, there will be more potentially operational engines than the fuel supply can support.

In that circumstance neither the capacity to produce new machines, nor the skill of the maintenance engineers, can change the number of machines that can be kept operational. Then, unless production is greatly reduced, a surplus of machines will have to be stockpiled or abandoned. All this consideration applies equally to the animal 'machine' with mating as the production line, and medical practice as the equivalence of maintenance engineering. The essential difference is the need for the biological internal combustion system to be kept 'ticking over' at all times if it is to remain a functional 'machine'. Thus, when there is no fuel to keep it going, the biological machine dies and disintegrates.

One other factor that determines the number of operational machines, when the fuel supply is finite, is the size of the engines. Generally speaking, the larger machines require more fuel than do the smaller ones per unit of operational time, and that fewer large machines than smaller machines could be kept running when there is a fuel shortage. Again, there is a parallel relationship: there never could be as many elephants as ants or rabbits. Human beings do not vary sufficiently in size for this to be a consideration, but they vary greatly in the amount of food they think that they need, and therefore take into their households, much of it being uneaten and wasted. When more is eaten than is being burned on a regular basis, this fuel accumulates as a fatty reserve that, in excess, is injurious. This differential between the under-indulged humans and overindulged ones is clearly a factor determining the magnitude of human population that the current world food supply can support. It also determines which individuals are most likely to die prematurely in the natural processes of equating population size and the food supply. The irony is that some premature deaths are the consequence of gross underfeeding, and others of gross overfeeding.

Unless the production of new units of human life is limited to the rate at which decommissioning is occurring, such that the human population size is kept comfortably within the limit of supportability, hunger for some is inevitable, and premature deaths will keep the population at that level. In other words, since the balance between birth and death must be sustained at the supportable level, if it is not achieved by birth limitation it will be achieved by death compensation. The neonatal human 'machine', being weak, and unable to search for and obtain fuel if not supplied to it, will be the most likely one to stall, and thus cease to be.

Because of this inevitable dependence of the size of the world population upon the extent of the world food supply, it is clear from the estimated changes in populations that have occurred in the course of the last 2,400 years (Fig. 3.1), that food supplies have been increasing progressively throughout that period. Evidently there was a slow and more or less linear increase in the food supply between 400 BCE and around 1600 CE. After that time there was a progressive increase in the rate of increase in food supply right up until about 1990. Since then the increase in population has continued, but now appears to have become a linear progression again. This could indicate a similar change in the rate of increase in food production. That could be bad news if it means that food production is now reaching a zenith. It could, however, be due, in part at least, to an increasing tendency of mated couples to opt for small families. That would be good news.

In this chapter, then, the considerations are firstly of the factors and processes that have accounted for the progressive increase in food production. Consideration is then of the state and sustainability of agriculture at the present time. The final consideration is of the need for even greater food production in the future to fuel the predicted substantial rise in a world population from 6 billion to 9 billion in the course of the first half of the twenty-first century. If that is achievable, it will then have to be sustained indefinitely at that artificially high level if a subsequent human population crash is to be avoided.

The Human Estate

The particular history of the human race is one of a progressive increase in its control of anything and everything upon which it can lay its hands, and over which it can exercise its will. That includes all other forms of life with which it shares the outer crust and atmosphere of planet Earth. In the course of this unrelenting pursuit of human benefit and advantage, mankind has tolerated and encouraged the proliferation only of those other life forms that are of some benefit to us, or which are pleasing to the eye, and cause us no harm. Mankind has sought to eliminate those life forms that are a direct or indirect threat to human well-being. Thus, through this increasing control over nature, mankind progressed from being gatherers of edible vegetation and hunters of herbivorous animals, to being cultivators of crops, and the managers of domesticated herbivorous mammals and birds, which convert inedible vegetable into edible animal tissue. The course of this early development of the control and increment of human food supplies is all but unrecorded. The shreds of evidence, however, indicate that both arable farming and sedentary and nomadic animal husbandry were developing in China, India and lands around the rivers Tigris and Euphrates some nine thousand years ago, and possibly even earlier.

Arable production of plants with edible seeds and fruits, and plants with edible roots, became progressively upgraded by the selection for cultivation of the species, and variants within species, which gave the highest yields in particular soils, and in particular climates. Alongside the selection of crops there was the progressive development of the means of preparing the soil for sowing, of irrigating, of harvesting, of the storing of edible parts of plants and of their preparation for human consumption. An important feature of developing agricultural systems was the storage of harvested produce so as to maintain its availability between harvests, and during periods of famine. Obviously human survival can depend as much upon the sustained availability of the food supply as upon the magnitude of seasonal yields.

Hunting was not only a way to supplement the food provided by the edible vegetation, but also to provide a continuous food supply during the seasons when a vegetable diet of edible fruits and roots was not available. The coexistence of arable farming and animal husbandry evolved, no doubt, as ways to sustain the availability of food throughout the year. Animals kept in association with arable cropping were additionally beneficial not only as the hauliers of ploughs to prepare the soil for crops, and as beasts of burden, but also as the providers of organic waste matter which helped to sustain the productivity of the soil. Nomadic animal husbandry was largely to harvest grassland vegetation that is inedible by humans. This is practised particularly where the quality of the soil or the seasonality of the precipitation rendered the land unsuitable for arable farming. Nomadic grazing prevents the overcropping and desertification that could result from the continuous cropping of smaller ranges. This provided a sustained food supply for the nomads, and a surplus of animals and animal produce which could be exchanged for other things the nomadic husbandmen and their families might need.

It was the progressive improvements and territorial extensions of this harnessing of vegetable and animal life forms for human benefit that resulted in the slow but progressive increase in food supplies that allowed particular populations to grow in size. Thus while a worldwide estimation of population changes indicates a steady increment in total food availability, the regional plots of population growth assembled by McEvedy and Jones (1978) indicate very different rates of increase in food production in different regions of the world. The Indian subcontinent, which was one of the spearheads in the development of agriculture, shows a much steeper increment in population and therefore in food production during the 2,000 years between 400 BCE and 1600 CE than elsewhere. That for North America shows a negligible change in population during that time interval, indicative of a negligible change in the productivity of the soil.

It was, of course, only where there was a progressive increase in the selection and management of plant growth, and in the controlled grazing of grasslands by domesticated species of herbivorous animals that populations could increase. The population increases were not, or not for long, limited to the expansion of rural communities directly engaged in arable farming and managed grazing. The bartering value of produce in excess of producer-needs created both an incentive to produce more than producer-needs, and an incentive to ensure that their own numbers did not rise to the extent that there was insufficient food either for themselves or for bartering. On the customer side of the market stall, the availability of food in exchange for goods, services or tokens, facilitated the creation of communities of craftsmen and traders that did not need to hunt for, or grow, their own food. Thus craftsmen and traders concentrated their businesses in convenient market settlements which grew into the urban concentrations of villages, towns and cities.

Food production thus evolved from an immediate necessity of families and tribes to improve food supplies for themselves, into an industry the activities of which became progressively more motivated by market forces. The urban dwellers were wholly dependent for their sustenance upon the marketing of the produce of farmers and herders; and the farming communities became dependent on the craftsmen for the manufacture of many items for which they had need. The distribution of the total population increase was determined by the extent to which increases in food production were shared, through trading processes, between the rural and the urban communities. Because of the increasing market opportunities it is difficult to know whether, at any particular point in the evolution of agriculture, agriculture productivity was being urged on by an increasing urban demand, or whether the expansion of urban communities was being facilitated by increasing agricultural productivity. There has always been, from the earliest occurrence of a division between agricultural and non-agricultural labour, a spiralling feedforward/feedback interaction between rural and urban communities, with each providing impetus to the other, and each needful of the other to sustain it. What can be said with reasonable certainty is that agriculture management, geared to producing an ever-increasing production of food in excess of that needed by the rural communities, has enabled an ever-increasing number of persons to make their livelihoods in other ways.

Thus from early in its history agriculture has provided food for more than the agricultural community itself, with the distribution of the surplus amongst non-agricultural communities being based upon trading transactions. This means that except for charitable distributions of food that is in excess of what can be disposed of by trading, distribution has always been according to the ability to pay for the food, rather than upon the urgency of the need for food.

Freedom from the prime need to search for or to produce food freed up increasing proportions of society to develop other crafts and, in time, indulge in all manner of learning about mankind per se and all aspects of the environment within which we live and upon which we depend. This included the material nature of the Earth's crust, and of the means by which metallic and non-metallic minerals could be extracted and employed for human benefit. Improved tools for manufacturing facilitated improved lifestyles. Maybe then, as now, the urbanites with their elaborate and somewhat artificial lifestyles, looked askance at the labourers on the land. They were, and still are, forgetful of the fact that everything about the continuity of urban human life rests four-square not only upon the products of the agricultural industry, but also on the ability to pay for them.

A consequence of the commercial basis of food distribution is that the sizes of regional populations, and the extent to which premature death is the population controller, may depend not only upon the regional food production, but also upon the ability of the community to buy in food from elsewhere. This dependency upon buying power extenuates the differentials in food distribution across the globe. Economically advantaged communities, tribes or nations can expand their numbers beyond that which their own agricultural endeavours could support, by purchasing food from elsewhere. When there is insufficient food on the international market to meet demand, it is the more affluent purchasers who remain adequately supplied, because market prices rise when supplies are inadequate to meet demand. The less affluent communities must then rely even more upon their own productivity, and most likely go hungry. There is then the risk that, rather than passively accept the miseries of a population crash, those in greatest need will resort to aggression as the only escape route open to them. In such circumstances they may feel compelled to seek vacant possession of neighbouring lands should their aggression succeed. Hence the needs of tribes to be able to defend their land and themselves against the ever present risk of an attempted take over, and to have belligerent capability when compelled to attempt a takeover. A consequence of this is that a proportion of the non-food-producing components of society is likely to be a militia maintained by the community for either aggression, or defence against aggression.

Many, if not most, intertribal conflicts are ultimately about land for food production; and most of the associated acts of genocide are to gain the benefit of possession, and preferably the vacant possession of the conquered territory.

From about the end of the seventeenth century CE or thereabouts, the human population started to grow at a progressively increasing rate. This became a near-exponential rise which continued almost until the end of the twentieth century. The rise continues into the twenty-first century but has now become fairly linear. This dramatic rise in human numbers can only be the result of a sustained increase in the world's food supplies of similar dimension. The overall upward progressions of food production and population, expressed in terms of worldwide population changes, conceals great regional variations in these progressions. These are due to different rates of change in agricultural technologies, to migrations in the wake of global voyages of discovery, and to the outcomes of military and economic struggles for land, with the advantages that conquests bring to the victors. Some of these territorial expansions have been between competing tribes within the same continent, while others occurred as the maritime nations competed in the occupation of distant new-found lands.

First and foremost in the change from a slow linear growth in population to a geometric rate of growth was Europe, where the change was preceded by an increase in the rate of the linear growth. This increased rate of linear growth started at around 1000 CE. The change to a geometric rate of growth occurred during the course of the seventeenth century. World population followed the same upward curve simply because it was then dominated by that of Europe. The matters to be considered then are the changes in food production that caused these population changes, particularly in the course of the last 300 years.

This shift from a linear to a near exponential rise in the European population was well under way before the emergence of effective death-preventing medicine, which can be dated from 1796 when Jenner (1749–1823) introduced cowpox vaccination against smallpox. Contrary to the popular assumption that 'medicine saves lives', the change in the rate of population increase could not have been the consequence of the introduction of effective medicine acting alone. 'Saved lives' can only become 'sustained lives' if there is food enough to continue to support them. Nor could the demand for labour create the industrial revolution, which was under way by the mid-eighteenth century, be the prime cause of a population rise. The need for labour in the newly founded mill towns could be met, in the first place, only by drawing on labour from elsewhere. That 'elsewhere' was largely the surrounding countryside. A consequential reduction in the agricultural labour force could have resulted in a reduction in the availability of food in the urban markets. This would have impeded the progression of the industrial development.

It is evident, from the fact of the population changes, that the increased need for food to sustain 'saved lives' was met, at least to the extent that the population growth indicates, both by the industrialisation of agricultural methods, and by the importation of foodstuffs from the young colonial territories annexed by European nations. This, however, does not mean that it was made possible to sustain every life that medical treatment spared from premature demise. This crude statement of population growth gives no indication of how many 'saved lives' were still ended prematurely because there was insufficient food to sustain them.

To simplify the complex interaction of circumstances which account for this change in the availability of food, the prime factors can be divided into three principal components: i) overseas land acquisition and the development of agriculture in these new-found lands; ii) the introduction into Europe of such exotic crops plants as the potato from the South American altiplano, and maize from North America; and iii) the application to agriculture of the applied sciences of metallurgy and steam power upon which the industrial revolution was based.

The new-found lands of America and Australasia, and parts of Africa, added enormously to the production of cereals and meat, which could be transported by sea to European markets. The comforting mythology of colonisation was that most of these new-found territories were empty at the time of their occupation by European settlers. This was not truly so. The position was more that since the lands were agriculturally undeveloped, the sizes of the native populations were limited to how many could be supported by the natural supplies of sustenance. The native inhabitants, being still largely hunters and gatherers, had little perception of the need or incentive to bend nature to the exclusive benefit of mankind, and to the detriment of the natural competitors. The European invaders, or colonisers as they preferred to be considered, brought with them the capabilities needed for organised arable farming and the management of grazing and browsing for meat production. The driving force in these developments was not only the immediate needs of the settlers but, even more so, the European markets for the agricultural produce. Eventually and inevitably, the increasingly more intensive land usage created conflict with the natives, who saw no need or virtue in such changes and for their dispossession of their territories. With good reason, they resented the gross interference with their long-established lifestyles. As Chief Seattle of the Suquamish Indians is reputed to have said, at around 1850:

> The Earth does not belong to man. Man belongs to the Earth. All things are connected. Man did not weave the web of life; he is merely a strand in it. Whatever he does to the web he does to himself.

Those expatriate Europeans, who wanted to own the land and use it recklessly and carelessly to satisfy their own immediate needs and those of distant markets, were of a different philosophy, and believed in a God-given right to sweep all before them. The validity of this belief was drawn from Chapter 1 of the Book of Genesis:

> ….Be fruitful and multiply and replenish the Earth and subdue it; and have dominion over the fish of the sea and over the fowl of the air and every living thing that moveth on the Earth.

On the grounds that the natives were a different order of God's creation, the newcomers believed that they had authority to dominate them too. Thus when the natives, and their non-possessive philosophies, were found to be a hindrance to the possession of the land by the newcomers, and to its exploitation to satisfy, and to profit from, the eager, needful European markets, the natives were progressively displaced and largely annihilated. This happened alike to the Indians in North and South America, the Aborigines in Australia and the Maoris in New Zealand. These progressive, and usually ruthless takeovers of colonised territories are not generally described as genocidal, but there really is no other word for the fate of the majority of the dispossessed natives.

These colonisations were different from the earlier territorial expansions by Romans, for example, because the development of ocean-going ships and means of oceanic travel brought the four corners of the Earth within the reach of the colonising European nations. The treatment of the indigenous occupants of overrun lands had plenty of precedents, ranging from the accounts of the annihilation of tribes as part of land clearance in the Old Testament through to Stalin's ruthless agricultural revolution in the last century, and to the present time. There was the distinction that whereas most other genocidal takeovers of territories were motivated by the food needs of the invaders themselves, in the case of the European colonisation of overseas territories, the motivation was to satisfy European markets the colonisers had left behind. Once the colonisers of these distant territories were producing more food than they needed for their own increasing numbers, it was economically sensible to maximise the supply of food to needful European markets. In exchange, Europe supplied the colonies with all manner of manufactured goods. The overseas markets for the products of the industrial revolution in Europe increased the need for labour in Europe, and this increased the need for food. That increased the markets for the food produced in the colonies. With this readily available food from the colonies there was then little, if any, restraint upon European population expansion. Food production in North America and Australia, particularly, has stayed well above the domestic needs to satisfy their own rapidly increasing populations. They have, therefore, remained the major suppliers to needful overseas markets. This has been almost entirely on a 'cash and carry' basis, which has meant, and still means, that the exportable food does not, generally speaking, go to those communities with the greatest need to augment their own production of food, but to those best able to pay for it. It can be expected that in time the populations of the ex-colonial territories will expand until the food that they can produce will do no more than satisfy their own needs. Meanwhile, however, the export of foodstuffs is a crucial part of their economies. Thus there is a continuing interest in sustaining food production, but in keeping populations at levels which allow for export as well as for domestic consumption.

Because of this availability of food from overseas and the ability to pay for it, European population growths have not been greatly restrained by limitations in their own food production. A noteworthy point is that because the importations of food into Europe were largely from territories with food production in excess of their domestic needs, this importation did not reduce the food available to the inhabitants of the vending country. This is not always so. Many relatively poor countries, anxious to earn overseas incomes, now produce exportable crops, while producing and retaining insufficient food for their own domestic needs. The suggestion that importing food from countries such as North America and Australasia involves no hardship elsewhere is not really true, for there are many parts of the world where hunger is endemic, and these areas might have been able to receive some of those exportable food surpluses were there not other ready buyers for them. To what extent European countries could be self-supporting if imported food was not available may have changed somewhat in recent years. When food importations into Europe became greatly restricted during World War II, Europe's own food production was only marginally adequate. Several European countries now claim to be self-sufficient, or even to have marketable surpluses, but most European countries are also importing food on a large scale. Britain, for example, while encouraging farmers not to produce more than they can sell, is importing up to 50% of its food. Maybe if all imports ceased, Britain would again find itself in much the same precarious position that it was in during World War II.

From the colonies of European countries there came not only new foodstuffs, but also the seeds of new foodstuffs, the introduction of which facilitated increases in European domestic food production. The best example of the introduction into Europe of new crops is the potato from the South American Andes in the sixteenth century. The great advantage of plants that store energy in their roots such as carrots, turnips, and potatoes is that a large proportion of the crop mass is edible by humans, especially when cooked to break down the cellulose cell membranes. That allows the ready digestion of the proteinous and starchy cell contents. The potato, being rich in carbohydrates, is a particularly valuable energy source. There is the further advantage that potatoes are easily grown and harvested in small quantities on small holdings such as cottage gardens, and do not require the processing that cereal crops need before being available as a food for humans.

The potato can thus provide a year-round basic human fuel supply, and cheaply so. Little wonder, then, that quite soon after its introduction it became, like bread, a basic nutritional provision.

The Irish Potato Famine in 1845, caused by a parasitic fungus, resulted in a human population crash. This was largely inevitable because the potato crop had become virtually the staple diet of the peasant classes. In consequence, when the potato harvest failed, alternative food supplies were insufficient. It is now evident that wheat grain was available in Ireland at that time, but the market was relentless, and there was then no OXFAM to bring grain to those who could not pay the market price. A lesson to be learned from that disaster is not so much the popularly accepted one of the danger of being dependent upon the ethics of a neighbouring tribe, but the danger of being dependent upon one particular plant species as the staple food provider. If the harvest should fail, and there is no alternative food supply, famine is inevitable. Another lesson, that we may be incapable of learning, is that the marketing of food as the means of its distribution ensures that, in famine conditions, it is the affluent sections of a community that are the survivors, and the poor that go under.

In Europe, agricultural practices had not changed dramatically at the time that population growth accelerated at an increasing rate, except for the introduction of the potato. Farms generally had remained small, and virtually all of them consisted of mixed arable cropping and livestock husbandry. This mixture ensured the input into the soil of water-holding humus, made of rotting cattle dung and straw. This also achieved the partial return to the soil of some of the minerals removed by the crops. Fallow periods also aided soil recuperation.

The rapid impact of the industrial revolution on agriculture was the improvements in farm machinery, especially the plough, and the means of hauling it through the soil, which facilitated deeper ploughing. Steam-powered vehicles also improved the transport of crops off the fields, and to the market, and provided machinery for the threshing of grain and for the milling of the separated seeds. In time, of course, the steam power was replaced by the oil- or petrol-driven internal combustion engine and the machinery became more manageable and had greater capabilities. Small fields then gave way to large fields better suited to mechanical farming technology, and crop farming and animal husbandry have now become largely separate farming specialities on separate areas of land.

Over the centuries preceding the seventeenth century many small agricultural improvements had contributed to the gradual increase in food productions and thereby in population sizes. The dramatic change in the rate of increase in agricultural productivity that then occurred was a consequence of the quite sudden codification of the accumulating knowledge of the nature of the substances of the Earth's crust, of their transformability; and of the forces by which the energy released by some of these transformations could be used to do useful work. Parallel to this accumulation, integration and codification of knowledge based on observation and experimentation, was the application of this knowledge to meet human needs and assist human tasks. Knowledge gained by observation and experimentation had been applied to practical purposes many times before the industrial revolution. The observed relationships between Earth and other heavenly bodies were applied to navigation of the seas, and to knowing when to sow and to reap crops, long before the nature of these relationships was accepted as valid by Europeans theologians. This earlier application of knowledge, however, was of a quite different order of significance to that which occurred from the seventeenth century onwards. The combustibility of coal extracted from the Earth's crust, and the use of the energy released as heat to create a pressure that could be used to drive machinery was to change everything in Europe and then in the world. It led to the replacement of the use of windmills and waterwheels to drive the mechanical devices in factories and mills; to the replacement of transport by the horse and cart and canal boats with the steam locomotion; and to the mechanisation of much of farming. This labour-saving method of speeding up the management of arable land and its crops came at a time when labour was drifting away from the land and into the industrial towns where a workforce was needed.

The mechanisation of agriculture was thus timely, and prevented a collapse of both agriculture, and of the new power-based industries, the one through lack of labour, and the other through lack of food. At the same time, the industrial revolution created welcome markets for the rising agricultural productivity of the European settlers in the 'new-found lands', particularly those of North America and Australasia. To a large extent, then, it was the market force of an expanding host of industrial workers that spurred and financed the mechanisation and expansion of agriculture both in Europe and Europe's newly acquired colonies. This increasing agricultural productivity also allowed the spread of industrialisation across Europe, and then soon after, to other regions of the world, and so to a more widespread population explosion.

As was explained in Chapter One, the end of World War II saw the introduction of the massive life-extending effects of disease control by antibiotic substances, and of insecticidal agents that acted on the vectors of human microbial diseases. It was realised by some that such massive interference with the occurrence of early deaths would provide the tendency for populations to increase rapidly, but that this would occur only if there was a concurrent and matching increase in the availability of food to sustain an escalating population. If that did not occur, then lives 'saved' by the application of the rapidly developing medical sciences would be negated by a rise in other causes of death directly or indirectly resulting from starvation. Since, however, food goes preferentially to those who can afford to pay for it, and since the benefit of these medical advances would be enjoyed first and foremost by the economically most advantaged populations of the industrialised countries, it was likely that any rise in the incidence of hunger and of premature deaths would fall not upon those benefiting most from the medical advances, but on those less economically favoured communities that could not buy in additional food to support any rise in population.

Thus, while the direct effect of new medical treatments would be to extend many lifetimes, the chances were high that without an agricultural revolution parallel with that in medicine, the overall death rate would not be reduced. The benefit would be for the more opulent societies, while the less opulent ones would suffer. The use of insecticides to combat malaria and other tropical diseases which are most prevalent in economically disadvantaged communities, could likewise fail to achieve the widely presumed benefit. Where there is no additional food for a community in which the death rate is lowered by effective malaria control, there would be a compensating rise in deaths with other causes, including hunger per se.

The Green Revolution

The second half of the twentieth century saw a rapid increase in food production now popularly known as the 'Green Revolution'. It was this that made it possible for 'saved lives' to be 'extended lives' without someone else somewhere else necessarily having to suffer. While, as individuals, we may know that our lives have been sustained by modern medicine, the accelerating overall growth in human numbers is not the consequence of medical advances, but of agricultural advances. Medicine, as stated earlier cannot, by itself, give rise to an increase in the number of persons alive at any time. It can only influence which individuals are afforded the chance to survive for longer.

Since there has been no evidence of a temporary halt in the

rapid rise in world population in the second half of the twentieth century, it is tempting to conclude that as a result of the Green Revolution, food production has continued to be adequate for human needs, and there have been no population crashes. The rise in population, however, was not because hunger had been eliminated or even contained. It was because an increasing food supply had allowed populations to increase, but still with much hunger, and with premature death as the principal effector of the balance between worldwide food production and the overall human population of the world. As was pointed out in Chapter three, the proportion of the world population suffering hunger to some degree may have always been of the order of 20%, and has continued to be so throughout the twentieth century. If this is a reasonably valid assessment of the incidence of hunger, and there is good reason to suppose that it is, it follows that the number of hungry persons has escalated as the world population has escalated.

This persistent and increasing hunger is not because the Green Revolution was insufficient, but because of the natural tendency for there to be more births than enough food for all newborn infants to be sustained through into maturity. While this circumstance prevails there will never be food enough to succour all and eliminate hunger as a substantial cause of premature deaths. More food means more infants surviving into sexual maturity. That results in more mating couples a few years hence, and an increased rate of childbirth. It is inevitable, then, that unless population growth is voluntarily checked, this upward spiral in worldwide hunger will continue, whatever the rate of increase in food production. When food production peaks, as sooner or later it must, population will then also cease to increase further irrespective of the birth rate. This population control will be executed by an increased incident of hunger-related mortality until a balance between birth rates and death rates is re-established at whatever population level the food supply can support. If the prevailing rate of food production then proves to be unsustainable, and begins to decline, the population must then also decline. Again, this will inevitably be effected by an increase in the rate of premature deaths; but almost certainly it will be augmented by the belligerent activities of individuals, families and tribes, as they seek to ensure their own survival at anyone else's expense. Such a population crash will be an exceedingly painful event either to witness or endure.

Since the rapid rise in population during the last half-century is evidence that food production had increased rapidly, and since such rapid changes in food production do not occur naturally, the matter now to be considered, is how it was that since the end of World War II in 1945 the increases in food production was such that the world population trebled from 2,000 million to 6,000 million between 1945 and 2000.

By the mid twentieth century there was little uncultivated land suitable for arable farming, at least in Europe. Most of the land which could be used for arable cropping had been ploughed up by the advent of the twentieth century, and during World War II (1939–1945) even pasture land and hill land previously considered unsuitable for arable crops was pressed into arable service. Since then, elsewhere in the world many forest areas have been cleared and used for arable cropping. Only with careful management, however, do such newly developed crop lands become and remain productive for more than a few years. Where the topsoil has little depth it can be blown away by wind or washed away by rainfall once it is denuded of trees. The soil may then become agriculturally useless. Furthermore, in the course of the last half-century great changes have occurred in agricultural practices. Regional separation of arable and livestock farming has became progressively more general, and arable farmers have preferred larger fields, which can be ploughed, prepared, seeded and harvested more economically using larger agricultural machinery. A disadvantage has been the loss of hedgerows which, by serving as windbreaks, reduce moisture loss from the soil, and the wind-borne loss of dried-out topsoil. It also meant that without nearby livestock farming there was no farmyard manure to sustain the fertility of the arable land. Thus in regions specialising in arable farming there was no alternative but to use inorganic fertilisers if eventual soil exhaustion was to be avoided, and if productivity was to be sustained and increased. Although inorganic fertilisation can completely replace the minerals that are lost from the soil when crops are sent to market, it cannot sustain the structure and water-retaining quality of soils, as does the application of organic residues such as farmyard manure. With the genetic selection of high-yielding grain, the application of inorganic fertilisers in quantities well above that need just to replace the minerals removed from the soil, the use of irrigation from waterways and aquifers, the use of insecticides and fungicides to prevent crop damage, and the use of selective herbicides to maximise the growth of the preferred vegetation, the yields, especially of grain crops, rose dramatically. Between the years 1950 and 2000 world grain production increased by more than two and a half times from some 700 million tons per annum to 1860 million tons per annum. It was this multifaceted revolution in arable agricultural productivity that has provided the means by which human populations could increase.

Agriculture, being a commercial enterprise, was responding to market forces. Without a growing market for agricultural produce, the capital investments would not have been made in plant breeding, agricultural engineering, irrigation systems and the mineral fertiliser industry to the extent that they were in the second half of the twentieth century. This market pressure was a feedback influence upon the agricultural industry of increasing populations, created initially by medical advances that postpone death, but were then sustained by the feedforward effect of increased food production. Thus there was a spiralling feedback/feedforward relationship between agricultural productivity and population size, with populations increases spurring the agricultural industry to greater productivity, and the increased agricultural productivity spurring the growth of populations. As ever, and as nature decrees, populations grew as far and as fast as the increasing food supplies allowed them to, with premature mortality remaining the principal adjuster of populations sizes. As has already been stated, while the degree of hunger varies both geographically and temporally, it would seem that seldom, if ever, has less than a fifth of the world's human population been severely undernourished. Thus, during the second half of the twentieth century, during which time the world population rose from some 2,500 million to 6,000 million – which increase closely parallels the increase in grain production – it is likely that the incidence of hunger has increased from some 500 million to 1,200 million persons. That number of people going to bed hungry each night is a fearful price to pay for the freedom to reproduce willy-nilly. It is no use believing that further increases in food production will alleviate the situation. It will not.

One can, of course, concentrate the mind on the other side of the coin, and argue that if the prerequisite of happiness is a full belly, then the opportunity for happiness has also grown at the same rate that the total population has grown, and that now some 4,800 million people enjoy that prime ingredient of happiness. That, however, might seem a selfish and heartless way of considering the present relationship between world population and world food supplies.

The Prospects

The matter now to be considered is not so much where we are now, as where we will be in only fifty years' time if the population/food supply and food supply/population interactions are allowed to continue their upward spirals. For the present world population of six thousand million to stay at this unnatural level, and with the present level of hunger and premature deaths, the present level of food production must be maintained. For reasons to be considered later, it is by no means certain that this will be possible.

Because there are six thousand million human beings alive today, with some of them grossly underfed, and others grossly overfed, it is self-evident that the current level of food production is adequate to support that number of human beings, and that it could support more of us, albeit in less comfortable circumstances for some of us, if the world's food was to be equitably distributed. That, however, is an impractical proposition, because the distribution of agricultural produce has always been by commercial means. Food is sold preferentially to those able to pay the market price, which depends on the forces of supply and demand. It is also impractical because better feeding would lead to an increase in population, and in consequence hunger would reappear. Whenever such a revolution has been attempted, with distribution being determined according to need rather than according to wealth, it has failed. This is at least partly because without the profit incentive, production falls and hunger increases.

With six thousand million human beings to feed at the beginning of the twenty-first century, two matters need urgent consideration. One is whether the present level of agricultural productivity can be maintained indefinitely, and therefore whether the present level of human population can be sustained. The other is whether the level of agricultural productivity can be further increased in the course of the next half-century, and so facilitate the increase of the human population to 9 billion or thereabouts, which is what demographers are predicting. If that 50% increase does occur it will create massive sociological problems, such as those of greatly increased urbanisation; even more stress on material resources, particularly water, and other harmful effects of efforts to further intensify food production. It would seem that the demographic predictions, achieved by extrapolation from the present rate of population growth, contain little consideration of the likelihood that it will be possible to feed 9,000 million persons in the year 2050 and thereafter. The prediction that when the world population has reached that number it will then level out lacks any indication of how it is supposed that the levelling out will occur. There are only two ways. Either humanity will make an all-out effort to keep its numbers at a level at which all can be fed, or the natural process of population limitation will do what has to be done. That, of course, is by the early elimination of those that are grossly underfed. What, then, is the prospect of avoiding a human population crash if the human population continues to rise as is predicted? It does not seem to be very good. The popular assumption is that human ingenuity will provide the means to overcome the pending population crash. The Earth's resources, however, are finite, and ultimately the size of the human population can only be that which an over-exploited Earth can still support. It is not in humanity's interest to move unchecked to the brink of that abyss, and then suffer the agonies of the crash.

The statistical information supplied in the annual publications of the Worldwatch Institute, *The State of the World* and, *Vital Signs*, indicates that the processes that have accounted for the first Green Revolution, during the second half of the twentieth century, may now have reached their zeniths. Not only may it not be possible, by these means alone, to continue to increase food production, but it may not even be possible to sustain the present level of food production. Using world grain production as a crude index of agricultural productivity, the data provided in the Worldwatch Institute's annual publication, *Vital Signs* shows that after a steady rise in world grain production between 1960 and 1998, it then flattened out, and now appears to have started a slow decline.

There may be more than one reason for this decline, including soil deterioration and failing supplies of water for irrigation; but a fall in demand on the international grain market could also be a factor. A fall in demand, however, might reflect an inability to pay for needed grain, rather than a reduction in the need to import grain. In this regard it is noteworthy that the amount of grain available per person on earth has been slowly but steadily declining over the last decade. The world grain carry-over stocks, expressed as the number of days the stock would last if not replenished, has also been declining. At something under 60 days, this is below the food security threshold, which has been set at 70 days. It is possible that the matter of immediate concern is not how to further increase food production, but how to sustain world food production at its current level.

There is little prospect of substantially increasing the amount of land under the plough. The Siberian steppes remain largely undeveloped, and some have wondered whether something similar to the opening up of the North American prairies could make Russia east of the Urals more productive agriculturally. The soil in Siberia is, however, less fertile, and the climate is more severe, than in the North American grain belts. Previous attempts to develop Siberia agriculturally have not been very successful. As with the clearance of forested land in the Amazon basin in South America, the clearance and ploughing up of the Siberia steppes would probably be of only short-lived benefit. To sustain and extend food production agriculture must look for indefinitely sustainable means of doing so. Because population follows food supply, unsustainable stopgap increases must, in the long term, cause more human suffering than they relieve in the short term.

Increased applications of inorganic fertiliser dressings played a crucial role in the Green Revolution during the second half of the twentieth century, by greatly increasing in grain crop yields. Further increases in inorganic fertiliser application, however, no longer have a substantial, and economically viable, augmentative effect. The cost of any increase in yield to be achieved by heavy dressing is greater than the financial return when the slightly higher yield is marketed. Even if this were not so, there is a heavy price to pay for the heavy use of inorganic fertiliser, which is the contamination of subterranean aquifers, not only with these applied minerals, and also with the still toxic residues of the insecticides, fungicides and selective herbicides with which soils are prepared or crops are dressed. Such contamination of aquifers does not necessarily have a negative feedback effect on crop yields, but many of the contaminated aquifers also supply water drunk by humans, and this can have serious health consequences. This is especially so when some of the chemicals accumulate in the body causing irreversible pathological effects. If this seepage of the chemicals used in agricultural into the aquifers could be stopped right now, it would almost certainly be too little too late, for it is estimated that the natural flushing out of some aquifers could take hundreds of years.

Additional to the growing problem of aquifer contamination there is increasing evidence that water is being extracted from many subterranean aquifers at rates well in excess of that of their recharging. This threatens the extent to which irrigation can be maintained as a means of sustaining current crop yields, let alone of increasing them. Furthermore since the water used for irrigation, whether from aquifers or surface waterways, is seldom if ever wholly free of mineral salts, irrigated lands are becoming increasingly encrusted with salts left behind when the applied water evaporates. Most current crop plants upon which humans rely for their food production do not flourish in salty soils. This also is casting doubt on the prospects of sustaining both the qualities and quantities of crops.

All things considered, the indications are that food production based on the technologies of the Green Revolution has reached its limit and may, because of the side effects of these technologies, be set for a gradual decline. It would thus seem that only a second 'green revolution' based upon developments beyond those of the first Green Revolution will be needed to provide adequate food for all the present six billion of us. Such a second green revolution will certainly have to occur for the human population of the world to grow to half as much again during the next half-century.

The only known likelihood of that is the genetic manipulation of crop plants to render them more suited to the variety of climates and the variety of soil conditions which occur naturally, and which are being created by human exploitation of the Earth's crust. The development of plant species, and varieties of species, that can thrive in salt-contaminated soils; or are resistant to drought, frost, wind damage, fungal infestation or insect predation; or which can add rather than remove nitrogen from the soil, – to mention only some of the possibilities of genetic engineering – could change the prognosis greatly. Much is already within reach. In China, for example, a genetically modified variety of rice promises a substantial increase in crop yields. Such an increase is greatly needed there, but without concurrent and adequate population limitation, the benefit of more rice would be only a short-lived respite.

It is too early to foretell how far it will be possible to augment world food supplies by human intervention using genetically modified plants; and it is too early to know whether such increased yields that are obtained by such means will be indefinitely sustainable. Some insuperable limitation to what the soil can yield could yet frustrate the hopes of salvation through a second green revolution. What we can be certain about is that this escalation of food production and with it, of human populations, cannot continue indefinitely. There must be a limit to the physical dimension of agriculturally usable land; to the capture of solar radiation by plants; to the water available for irrigation, and to the extent that increases in soil mineral contents can enhance plant growth. All are finite, so if these new agricultural endeavours are allowed to fuel further uncontrolled population rises, mankind will be buying time, but not using it wisely. Without stabilising the balance of population and the sustainable level of food production, a population crash become inevitable, sooner or later.

Many will not wish to believe this prognostication, but having no substantial grounds upon which to dispute it, they may resort to the argument that future problems are for future generations to resolve as best they can. Hedonism today, for those more privileged persons who are able to know it, must not, it seems, be spoiled by concern for the future – even for that of one's own grandchildren. Many others, it seems, are able to convince themselves that being a special and favoured creation, some divine intervention can be relied upon to spare mankind from the disastrous consequences of its own folly. In the absence of any conclusive evidence of the validity – or the invalidity – of supernatural interventions that avert human tragedies, it might be more provident to assume, at least as a working hypothesis, that we are by ourselves. It could be that the survival or demise of some human germ lines, and even of the entire Homo sapiens germ line, depends upon our willingness and ability to take control of an increasingly serious situation. What can we do? We are, it seems, now beginning to accept the need to refrain from laying our hands on anything and everything of the Earth's crust for our immediate benefit and gratification. There are still influential leaders – mostly theological leaders – proclaiming that to deliberately keep our numbers at that level at which all can be adequately fed is *contrary to the will of their deity*. Hunger and conflicting theological dogmas are, and have long been, the principal causes of human conflict. The humanist, by contrast, sensitive to the misery of widespread hunger, and aware of the added miseries of conflicts that hunger can give rise to, finds the opposition to population control difficult to appreciate. One can only argue the humanitarian case for population control, loudly and clearly, and hope that one is heard.

Genetically Modified Crops

The point is made in the above section that without wilful population control and without a second 'green revolution', there can be little realistic hope of stemming the rising tide of regional hunger, and the resultant high incident of premature death. The point is also made that the only prospect of effecting a major advance in food production is by the controlled genetic modifications of food-yielding plants to counter present limitations. This, considered in the context of the worldwide equation of populations and their food supplies, the principle of employing genetically modified crops to boost agricultural productivity, would seem to be irreproachable. The advocacy of research into genetic engineering of agricultural crops, as the only escape route from ultimate human disaster, is not to deny that, like many medical procedures, the therapy recommended may not be devoid of an element of risk. Regarding the medical analogy, one enquires what the risk is, and whether the risk of the therapy is greater or less than the risk of rejecting it. Only then can one decide whether to accept the offered treatment of the ill. Furthermore, in reaching that conclusion one might consider not just one's own self-interest, but also that of others who are likely to be affected by the decision one makes.

The present – almost hysterical – panic, in Europe particularly, over the introduction of genetically modified (GM) foodstuffs, is now spreading, as hysteria does, even to regions where regular or periodical famine is a fact of life. In a letter to the *New Scientist* (15 February 2003), Alex Avery of the Hudson Center for Global Food Issues tells that in 1999 the Zambian government rejected genetically modified food aid donated by the USA, and preferred that its citizens starved. A desperate mob took their future into their own hands and 'liberated' 230 tonnes of modified US corn which was being denied to them. In the absence of any confirmed evidence of the harmful consequences to mankind, either directly or indirectly, the decision by the European Commission in 2003 to uphold the de facto moratorium on both the production and importation of GM crops into Europe could be a harmful reaction in more than one sense. Not only will this prejudice against GM technology be likely to increase the pains of hunger worldwide by the denial of means of increasing food production, but as Helleman (2003) has pointed out, the cancellation of GM research in Europe in response to consumer fears, will put Europe well behind the USA in this area of applied science. Much of this fear is engendered by apparently authoritative utterances from high places. Thus the erstwhile British environment minister Michael Meacher wrote, in 2003, 'We have been feeding ourselves perfectly adequately since overcoming problems of hunger in our early existence. GM is not necessary'. That only makes any sense if 'We' refers to us in the UK, where widespread hunger need not exist because copious food imports can be afforded. It sounds like someone viewing his own backyard, and seeing that all is well there, concludes that all is well with the world. It is a preposterously erroneous, misguided and misguiding utterance of the 'I'm all right, Jack' variety.

It must be conceded that there is at least the possibility that alien genetic material introduced into a genome to create a phenotype favourable to producers and/or consumers of the vegetable, might not be as firmly integrated into the host genome as is hoped and intended. The added DNA sequence could, perhaps, detach itself from the gene complex in which its addition has a beneficial consequence, and append itself to the gene complex of another organism where its addition could have harmful consequences. Since gene-swopping can occur also between unmanipulated genomes, while disastrous occurrences attributable to such genetic changes are rare, the popular anticipation and fear of such occurrences if GM crops are used to increase food production seems to be disproportionate to the quite remote likeliness of serious problems. In contrast, the high risk of inducing a carcinogenic mutation from tobacco smoking is happily taken by millions of people. Likewise, influenza, which kills some 700,000 persons every year, could, at any time, by spontaneous mutation or by gene transgression, give rise to a truly catastrophic epidemic. Yet vaccination against influenza is taken up by only about half of those to whom it is offered. As is pointed out in the *New Scientist* (10 January 2004, p.19) much could and should now be done to enhance the efficacy of the influenza vaccine, but is not being done. This is largely because there is no clamour for it to be done.

It is odd that there is so little concern about these known hazards of tobacco smoking and the influenza virus, yet such widespread alarm over the much more speculative hazard of growing genetically modified crops. Means must be found to increase world food production at least to that extent needed for the continuing rise the human population. The failure to do so is to invite a far more fearful and disastrous human population crash than those already occurring regionally and with increasing frequency. It is now well established that GM technology can be used to counter many of the consequences of past human mismanagement of the soil, and to sustain and increase the yields of food crops. It is, as has been recently pointed out by the Nuffield Council of Bioethics (see *The Observer*, 28 December 2003), a moral duty of Britain, for example, to fund the pursuance of GM research. Those who are opposed to this are acting selfishly in the dubious belief that they are thereby protecting themselves, but are evidently heedless of what suffering such restrictions on progress may mean to others.

While the European Commission decided in March 2003 to uphold the de facto moratorium on both the importation and production of GM foods, McFadden (2002) has pointed out that the technology required to manipulate the genomes of crop plants is already beyond the control of 'Western' governments generally, let alone of Europe. It is also now largely outside any monopoly control by the international agrochemical giants. The use of genetically modified (GM) crops to increase food production where it is most needed is now virtually unstoppable. GM rice, for example, is already being used extensively, and it is contributing to the resolution of the problem of adequately feeding the 3,000 million humans, half the total world population, for whom rice is the staple grain. It was, for example, announced in 2002 that when a pair of genes of a bacterium are added to rice, this enables the plant to produce the sugar trehalose. This allows the plant to thrive in salty, drought-ridden or cold soil. The activity of the added gene is turned on only when the plant becomes stressed by these adverse conditions. It is hoped that this genetic modification will do the same and may also do the same when introduced into the genomes of other cereals.

Fortunately, while Europe nervously cogitates, promising progress is being made elsewhere towards a GM-based second green revolution which is encouraging. It must also be borne in mind, however, that the relief from hunger that GM technology could offer could be only a short-lived reprieve unless adequate steps are taken to hold the consequential rise in the human population in check.

Almost too late to include in these comments on the application of GM technology to food production, is the 2004 report of the Advisory Committee (to the UK Government) on Releases to the Environment. This recommends that certain GM crops should be allowed to be grown, but only for animal feed. This is a cautious advance, but its acceptance will still rest largely upon public opinion, which will determine whether the GM crops can be marketed.

The Advisory Committee's verdict relates, it seems, not so much to the possibility of deleterious gene migration as to the possibility that crop plants rendered resistant to otherwise wide-spectrum herbicides could result in gross disturbances to the ecosystem. Indeed, a recent study of this likelihood showed lower counts of invertebrate organisms in the soil on which GM crops had been grown than in soils on which the non-GM breeds had been grown. This result was not because of the quality of the GM varieties per se, but because the genetic modification allowed a different herbicide treatment. This did not prevent the anti-GM lobby greeting the result as a vindication of its hostility. Actually the environmental effects of different herbicide treatments of crops could be a matter of application technique. In a similar study with GM and non-GM sugar beet the altered beet provided a haven for wildlife (see *New Scientist,* 18 January 2003), and this was apparently because of the way that the herbicide was applied.

There is an element of naivety in this concern over the possible consequences of growing GM crops. This is partly because very much the same genotypic, and thereby phenotypic differentials between strains of crop plants could possibly be achieved by orthodox plant breeding, although that may take somewhat longer to effect. Another consideration is that everything one does in agriculture to increase yield changes, or is likely to change, the prevailing ecosystem. This change has been progressive ever since the dawn of agriculture some 9,000 years ago. Arable agriculture is basically the replacement of a naturally occurring complexity of plant and animal life forms, with as near as human ingenuity can get to the monoculture of a plant of particular human usage. To that end all other plants become designated as weeds. Each step in that progression has entailed the further destruction of the erstwhile natural plant ecology, and therefore of the natural animal ecology.

Thus every recent advance from deep ploughing, inorganic fertilisation, selective vegetation control (weed killers), selective fauna control (e.g. pesticides), the creation of hedgerows as windbreaks and as barriers to animal migration, to the removal of hedgerows to accommodate modern agricultural machinery, has caused substantial, but largely unrecorded, changes to already quiet unnatural ecosystems. This is not to say that changes in supra- and intra-soil changes in life forms other than the selected crop plant have not sometimes had effects that would have been better avoided. It is to say that such research reports, as those being discussed here, need to be put into realistic and historical perspective. Mankind changes anything and everything about ecosystems whenever it suits it to do so. It is well to remember that had it not done so there would not now be 6,000 million of us, each primarily concerned only with personal well-being.

In a thoughtful and responsible leader article in the *New Scientist* (14 June 2003) it is concluded that in the absence of any convincing evidence of the harm of GM crops, the question should not be whether or not GM crops should be grown, imported or eaten, but whether there is adequate control to protect both consumers and the environment. What is needed is good risk management, vigorous environmental monitoring, and the mandatory labelling of GM foodstuffs. Careful progression in the introduction of GM foodstuffs is surely the way to go. Meanwhile the UK could soon have problems. Bakers and consumers of bread prefer imported hard wheat grain to home-grown soft wheat grain, much of which is used as cattle feed. What is to be done when no wholly GM-free hard wheat grain can be imported?

Who Will Feed China?

A quite frightening aspect of the availability of exportable grain only to those able to pay the market price is to be found in Lester Brown's book *Who Will Feed China?* (1995). The gist of the text is that China has industrialised at an astounding rate, and to an astounding degree. Consequently much of China's quite limited agricultural land, relative to the size of the population, has been lost. Much of the water formerly used for the irrigation of crops has been diverted to meet industrial and urban needs, and erstwhile agricultural workers have migrated to the newly established industrial townships. Because of this, agricultural productivity has not expanded at the same rate as has the Chinese population, and China has become increasingly reliant upon grain imports. China's demands upon the international grain market are currently being met, because the foreign currency earned by China's expanding industrial exports allows China to purchase the grain it needs on the international market. So long as the grain can be paid for the transactions occur irrespective of whether or not there is greater need for the grain elsewhere. As the demand increases this is likely to cause a rise in the price of grain, which will cause hardship elsewhere in the world, where grain purchases are inadequate, but are all that can be paid for. That, however, is what capital-based market systems are all about: whoever has the purchasing power gets the goods, while those who are economically disadvantaged are compelled to do without.

There is the possibility that eventually so much of the grain available for export by the principal grain-producing countries will be purchased by China, that little or nothing will be left for others in equal or greater need. This shortage could preclude the distribution of food aid to the disadvantaged communities facing famine. If the time ever comes when this, or any other major grain purchaser is unable to get all the grain it needs by market trading, a dangerous political situation could arise. As was noted earlier, much of historical belligerency has arisen out of the need of tribes to increase their food supplies. This should warn us of what could happen if, in the future, a powerful nation needs a smaller nation's food supplies, and is compelled to consider the prospects of acquiring it by force.

Two other aspects of the industrialisation of China are noteworthy:

i) A Population Crash

Although there was no worldwide population crash in the second half of the twentieth century, there have been regional population crashes. Indeed, not withstanding the Green Revolution which allowed the massive increase in the human population, death as a direct or indirect consequence of hunger is an everyday event in one part of the world or another, and these famines are growing both in frequency and magnitude. In the absence of an adequate control of the birth rate, these are inevitable occurrences which are contributing to the natural population control by premature deaths. The greatest of these regional population crashes occurred in China during 1959 to 1961, when some 30 million persons died of starvation. Even against the background of a continuing rapid rise in population, deaths in China then greatly exceeded births. This occurrence shows up quite clearly on the plot by Lester Brown (1995) of the annual addition to the world population between 1950 and 1994 (Fig. 4.1). This crash was occasioned by the shift from an essentially peasant economy to an industrial one. Agricultural productivity fell while the market for agricultural products increased, and dire hunger resulted. This was an exceptional circumstance from which China rapidly recovered. Its population then continued to be fast growing. It does serve as a warning, however. If agricultural productivity goes into decline worldwide, a population adjustment must follow, and that is how, in nature, it will be done.

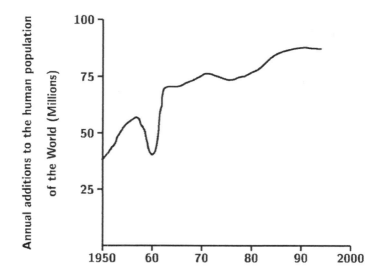

FIG. 4.1   THE ANNUAL ADDITION TO THE HUMAN POPULATION OF THE
WORLD BETWEEN 1950 CE AND 1995 CE (BASED ON A FIGURE BY L
BROWN, 1995)

ii) The Meat Culture

Homo sapiens, having lost the digestive system of an herbivorous
animal, and with only the vermiform appendix remaining as a
potently troublesome reminder of an herbivorous past, is now a
natural omnivore. When Homo sapiens was a gatherer and
hunter, edible roots and fruits provided a seasonal diet, and
animal flesh was the food supply of all seasons. Throughout most
of the history of managed food production, the essential role of
domesticated herbivorous animals has been to convert inedible
vegetation into edible substances. The domesticated animals thus
graze on grasslands which, for reason of terrain or soil structure,
are unsuitable for arable farming, or are grazed on arable land
during fallow periods. This latter usage provided the basis of
mixed farming by which both edible plant matter and edible
animal product were produced. At the same time the farm
animals benefit the crop farming by helping to sustain the soil
structure with their organic residue. With mixed farming, the

amount of animal products that can be produced is limited by the availability of grazing land.

The aim of the agricultural operative, like that of any other business person, is to maximise profit, which is most generally best achieved by producing what is most readily saleable in the market place. An increased demand for meat and dairy produce is a common indicator of raised living standards in successful industrialised communities. Hence the market pressure on the agricultural industries supplying industrialised communities to produce more meat and dairy produce. There was thus a search for ways to increase yields of beef, dairy produce, pork, poultry and fish. Since much of the harvested grain is deemed unsuitable for the manufacture of grain-based products for direct human consumption, a most successful solution has been to the feed grain to animals, and so produce enough animal products to meet the demand. In China, for example, as the economy has grown and the standard of living has risen, the demand for meat has risen. Thus much of the grain that China now purchases on the international market is not used to feed humans directly, but is fed to animals to increase meat production. In doing this the Chinese are only following a trend started in the United States, but is now more general in industrialised countries.

It takes 2 kg of grain to produce 1 kg of fish or poultry, 4 kg of grain to produce 1 kg of pork, and 7 kg of grain to produce 1 kg of beef. If the grain was truly surplus to human needs, its diversion to feed domestic animals and, incidentally, also to produce biofuel for automobiles, would be of no great consequence. That, however, is not the case. When grain is used on a large scale to produce animal products, there is less grain available for direct human consumption. It follows then, that fewer humans can be kept alive in a world 'hooked' on high meat consumption. Since, however, hunger has only a limited influence on the birth rate, if any at all, this cultural insistence on a high meat diet inevitably reduces the survival prospects of some newborn infants, particularly in the economically deprived regions of the world. Considered in this way, an over-indulgence on grain-based animal products in affluent communities has the tail-sting of contributing to the hunger that exists in the wider world. This will be evident when, as will surely happen one day, all the world's marketable grain has been sold to the highest bidders, and there is none that can be sent to relief famines amongst the peoples of poorer nations.

There are, even now, many hungry people who would be glad of this grain for direct human consumption; but it is of no concern of sellers in the market place what the purchaser does with the bought goods. Thus the grain producer is content to sell his wares to the meat producer so long as the price is right. That the grain is not then available for either commercial or charitable distribution to where it is most needed for feeding people directly is not the seller's concern.

The amount of grain now fed to animals is enormous. Data given in the Worldwatch Institute's *Vital Signs 2003* show that in the course of the second half of the twentieth century worldwide meat production increased fivefold from 44 million to 230 million tons. Over the same period the world population increased some 2½ times from 2.5 billion to 6 billion. This differential suggests that average meat consumption per capita rose considerably. Indeed, it did: the same data source gives the mean meat production per person as rising from 17 kg to 38 kg. A 2.5-fold increase in the meat per person over those fifty years, despite a 2.4 fold increase in world population, closely matches the fivefold increase in meat production. Since, however, it is likely that no more than 50% of the world population is enjoying the burgeoning opulence that goes with successful industrialisation, the increase in meat consumption by the better-off citizens of the world almost certainly increased much more than two and a half times over the last half-century.

Meat production in the year 2002 was of the order of 242 million tons. It is unlikely that less than 60% of this was from grain-fed animals. If it is assumed the grain-fed meat production was of the order of 150 million tons, and 4:1 is taken as the mean conversion rate of grain to meat, the amount of grain used to produce meat production could have been 600 million tons in the year 2002. The world grain production in that year is given, provisionally, as 1,833 million tons. Thus it would seem that more than 30% of the total grain production could have gone to the production of a luxury food rather than used as essential food.

Thirty per cent more grain available for direct human consumption could mean much to those who are hungry, and could have been the difference between life and death for many of them. But who, amongst big meat-eaters, really cares sufficiently to suffer a reduction in their own living standards? Even if enough did care sufficiently to effect a fairer food distribution of food, as already iterated and reiterated, without adequate birth control this would not be a lasting solution to the plight of hunger and resultant premature death.

Organic Farming

Residues of the chemicals sprayed onto soil or crops as herbicides, fungicides and selective weed killers can be harmful when they contaminate the produce and are ingested, or become present in drinking water. It is principally for this reason that there is a growing demand for what is called 'organically grown foodstuffs'. With the yearning that most of us have to live for as long as possible and to stay healthy for as long as possible, the popularity of the presumed, and much publicised, benefit of returning to traditional methods of farming is understandable. Whether or not the products of 'organic farming' are really more conducive of good health than are the products of modern intensive farming remains to be proven unequivocally. There is, however, a report (Halweil, 2003) of a study which provides support for the long-standing suspicion that the heavy use of pesticides and chemical fertilisers can disrupt the ability of plants to synthesize some of the secondary metabolites which may be necessary for the well-being of the plant, but are also important dietary additives conducive to human well-being. Thus organically grown plants have been found to contained more of the compounds which have antioxidant properties than were found in plants grown under other farming methods. Antioxidants such as these are believed to reduce the risks of human body malfunctions including cancer, stroke and heart diseases. It has yet to be shown that there is a difference in the incidents of these diseases between persons who always select organically grown foodstuffs, and those who decline to do so. Pending confirmation both of these experimental findings, and of a differential effects on human health, there is at least a good tentative reason why those who can afford to do so should prefer to eat organically grown products whenever the choice is available.

Having said that, it must be added that such possible benefits, may be accompanied by some dis-benefits. One is that the practices of 'organic farming' could also have health hazards. Another is that with an expanding market for 'organic' produce, and with suppliers anxious to benefit from it, there is scope galore for dishonest practices and mislabelling. There is as much need for vigorous control over the origin and quality of foods labelled as being organically produced, as there is over the added chemical residuals contained on or in the products of intensive agriculture. It is not a simple matter of 'black and white'.

What is abundantly clear is that only an economically advantaged section of society can be tempted 'to go organic' as a matter of principle. With truly 'organic farming', yields per hectare are unlikely ever to match those obtained by modern intensive farming practices, and for that reason the cost to the consumer of organically produced dietary items is unlikely to become competitive, when and where purchasing power is a prime consideration.

Amongst the notional benefits of organic farming is the well-entrenched belief of some that plants grow better when the minerals essential for growth are supplied to them as organic matter, than when they are supplied in the form of inorganic mineral molecules. This is more a tenet of faith than an evident fact, for plants cannot take up minerals other than in inorganic form. However the essential minerals are placed in the soil, they are not available for plant growth until they are broken down into soluble inorganic ions that the roots can absorb. There is potential benefit of organic matter for plant growth, but this is somewhat indirect. In drought conditions, the increased humus content of the soil facilitates water retention, and when rainfall is copious, soluble inorganic minerals may quickly leach away into the subsoil and into subterranean aquifers. This leaching will not occur to the same extent when the minerals are being released slowly from decomposing organic matter. Furthermore, depending on from where it is obtained, the application of organic matter to the soil will mean that the plants will not suffer from any of the harmful effects that added inorganic chemicals might cause, and the produce will not contain any residues of inorganic treatment. The humus content to the topsoil increases the soil's water-holding property. This is particularly beneficial when rainfall is interspersed with periods of drought. Thus, all else being equal and above board and the purse allowing, a strong case can be made for preferring a diet of organically grown produce, even while the evidence of benefit remains somewhat marginal. There are, however, two caveats which may – or may not – be considered to be of sufficient merit as to cause the customer to think again.

One caveat is that it is virtually impossible to return, as organic matter, all that is taken from the soil when plant material is being cropped and marketed. At least some of the plant growth is sent off the land, and permanently so. As market and population pressures compel the effort to produce ever-higher crop yields, the rate of loss of minerals from the soil increases. This would not be so if all consumer waste could be returned to the soil, as was the case with cottage kitchen gardens kept to supply family needs. The addition of the content of the receptacle in the small shed at the bottom of the garden, to the plant residue, allowed almost a 100% return to the soil of the mineral taken from it by plant growth. Modernisation of sewerage arrangements, and the urbanisation of as much as half of the population of the world, has rendered the return to the soil of anything like 100% of that which was sent to market quite impossible because of logistical complications, transport costs and the potential health risks of attempting to do so.

Where, then, do the 'organic farms' obtain all the organic matter needed to maintain the fertility of the soil? They cannot generate enough themselves, and therefore, other organic farms have likewise nothing to spare to pass on. It has been suggested that a considerable fraction of the mineral replenishment is by wind-blown minerals from neighbouring 'non-organic' farms. If so, this airborne mineral replenishment would surely somewhat violate the principles of organic farming. It is, then, very likely that organic residue is often obtained from other farms that use modern intensive farming methods with heavy inorganic treatment of the crops. Such farms might be willing to sell their organic residues for a good price, but must then rely more upon mineral fertilisation of their own soil and crops.

The only other major source of organic matter is sewage sludge, the great bulk of which derives from the urban human conurbations. This is used by 'organic' farmers where the redistribution costs are not prohibitive, but since there can be contamination both with heavy metals and potentially dangerous micro-organisms, the crops which depend upon sewage sludge may not be as healthy as the purchaser of organically grown foodstuffs supposes. Additionally it has recently been reported (see *New Scientist,* 20 April 2002, p.15) that when farm yard slurry is used as the organic mineral additive, it can contain the still active residues of antibiotic substances fed to farm animals to improve weight gain as much as to control infections. This contamination has been linked to the occurrence of antibiotic-resistant infections in humans consuming produce grown on land so treated. If this connection is confirmed it raises the possibility that the supposed health benefits of crops claimed to be unexposed to herbicides, fungicides, and pesticides, may be to some extent negated by the health hazards of organic soil fertilisation with sewage slurry and farmyard slurry. If personal safety is the principal consideration when buying organically grown foodstuffs, clearly the purchaser needs to know much more than just where it was grown.

The second caveat relates to the unlikelihood that the yield per acre of organically grown crops can equal that of modern intensive farming. There is the presumption in most of Europe and North America, that food is plentiful, and that reduced yields per unit of arable land as organic farming spreads is of no serious consequence. The validity of that presumption relates only to those favoured states where any shortfall in productivity could, if there is need, be resolved by importation from elsewhere. A worldwide perspective reads differently. Overall there is hunger galore, much of which the international food markets leave undressed because many nations cannot afford to pay for their needs. It must be added that if all those needful nations were given the wherewithal to shop around there would not then be sufficient stocks in the international marketplace to satisfy their demands.

The world grain carry-over stocks, (see *Vital Signs*, 1998) indicate how far the demand could be increased to empty the storehouses. Worldwide, the grain carry-over, which is now below what is considered as the safety threshold of 70 days, is a measure of the extent to which we live 'hand to mouth' and rely upon the prompt arrival of the next harvest, even without any serious attempt being made to resolve the current degree of hunger in the world. Although, therefore, organic-farming is spreading rapidly, it is not a universally applicable means of escape from the pollutions caused by modern agricultural methods. Nor can it contribute to the resolution of the overall problem of feeding the underfed.

Hence comes a great dilemma. Should we advocate organic farming because is will reduce the harmful effects of inorganic fertilisers, herbicides, pesticides etc., and because it may be beneficial to us, the well-fed half of humanity, regardless of its global impact? Or should we continue efforts to feed the now greatly inflated world population, regardless of the environmental damage and other unpleasant consequences which that could cause? There is no simple answer except that one which is decreed by our inherited instinct to put ourselves before the others when the crunch comes. Meanwhile, whatever the pros and cons of organic farming, its popularity will grow in affluent communities simply because it is seen as a means of effecting personal survival for as long as possible. The debate continues between the ardent advocates of organic farming and the cautious sceptics. Food produced by organic farming methods could well be a sensible choice for those who can afford that route, and who are unconcerned about the effects it could have on world food supplies. Others may see reason to have second thoughts.

Summary Comment

It is evident that except in unusual circumstances, population sizes are fixed by the availability of food, either home-grown or imported. One such unusual circumstance is when a large tract of agriculturally undeveloped land is acquired and turned to the managed production of food, as in Australasia and the Americas. For a while at least, there is far more food than the colonisers need for themselves, and the surplus is put up for sale. Another circumstance is found in Europe generally, where an economically buoyant but numerically stable society can buy in whatever additional food is needed to support an unnaturally high population density.

During the 2,000 years before the seventeenth century, there was a slow but progressive improvement in land management, which allowed a slow but progressive increase in food production, and thereby allowed a slow but progressive increase in regional population sizes. In the course of the seventeenth century food production in particular regions started to increase at accelerating rate with a consequential corresponding accelerating rise in regional human populations.

There are signs that food production by current intensive agricultural means is now somewhere close to its zenith. Little undeveloped land suitable for sustained cultivation remains for exploitation. Heavier applications of minerals to the soil no longer result in dramatic increases in crop yields. There is evidence that the present level of crop irrigation cannot be extended, and may already be unsustainable. Although demographers predict a rise of the world population from 6 billion to 9 billion within the next half-century, this will occur only if food production can be increased by some 50%, and can then be sustained at that yet further elevated level. The demographers do not explain how and why they predict that the world population will stabilise at around 9 billion. Without a positive endeavour to control population size, only the natural process of population limitation will operate. What this means is that those humans, and especially the neonatal humans, who cannot be adequately fed, will have short unhappy lives. The survivors will be those who manage to obtain enough food for themselves and their families in a highly, and probably brutally competitive, environment. We are genetically prepared for that: our instinct, like that of animals generally, is matched to that course of action. That animal instinct is to seek personal survival regardless of what that may mean to others.

Currently there must be enough food for the extant 6,000 million human beings, for otherwise that number could not exist. So long, however, as the balance between food production and human numbers is achieved by the premature deaths of those inadequately fed, hunger will be with us somewhere. A more equitable distribution of the food across the world would briefly relieve that situation, but would not be a durable cure. Likewise, producing more food can allow only a brief release from human hunger, since without population control, it will allow populations to grow until famine and premature death is again the population controller. The only way to avoid the spiralling of food production and population until food production can no longer be increased, is to limit human populations wilfully to that number which a sustainable level of food production can support.

As has been stated already, the attraction and the intentions of organic farming are to sustain the condition of the soil, the environment and human health. It is not intended to address, and does not address, the problem of reducing hunger in faraway places. Indeed, if practised on any scale beyond that of meeting the demands of small privileged communities, it would involve a reduction in food production, and consequently would be the cause of an increase in premature deaths and a reduction in the human population.

It is not yet possible to say whether or not the genetic modification of the genomes of food-producing plants to increase yields are as potentially harmful as some would have us believe. What is less debatable is the harm to humanity if a second green revolution is not achieved. The only prospect there is of providing food enough to feed a still increasing world population is by the application of GM. Those who oppose the development of this technology on grounds of fear for themselves might first reflect upon the many hazards of being alive, and try to put the GM fears into perspective. Those who do not want GM food production for fear that it would harm them, and do not approve of humane population limitation on specious philosophical grounds, should consider those who will inherit the Earth, as well as themselves. They should also consider whether human survival and welfare is best served by natural (instinctive) selfishness, or by a more humanistic attitude to others.

Chapter Five
TRIBALISM

The social history of mankind rests upon the instinct in each of us, as in animals generally, to survive for long enough to reproduce and to nurture our progeny. This survival depends upon achieving three primary conditions: 1) finding, aggressively if needs be, enough food for oneself and for one's still dependent progeny; 2) finding a mate, or mates, and breeding successfully; and 3) being able to protect oneself and one's still immature progeny from predation.

These conditions, which vary greatly between species, are essentially instinctive, with the survival of those gene lines best fitted to do so in any particular set of environmental circumstances. With many animals species the essentials of survival are achieved by individuals acting alone and exclusively in their own interests. Other species, particularly some of the predatory carnivores, have acquired the instinctive ability to collaborate in the capture of prey, and in mutual defence. Homo sapiens is, in strictly biological terms, a pack animal that lives in communities, and operates communally in the acquisition of food, in the defence of group territory and, when necessary, in the extension of territory by aggression. In the human species particularly, but not exclusively, this instinctive behaviour is overlaid with learned social behaviour with strong tribal connections. Thus tribalism is based upon inherent properties with many differing degrees and patterns of cultural development and sophistication, which are passed on from generation to generation by processes of instruction through example and learning. The operation of the basic survival instincts does not necessarily require any conscious direction. The order of consciousness that Homo sapiens possesses, however, provides an increased ability to select and direct the responsiveness to the environmental circumstances, to learn from past experiences, and to devise means of improving performance.

Most likely it was an ancestral elaboration of the means of catching prey, and of defending and acquiring territory, that evolved into the social behaviour patterns of human tribal societies, with the collaboration and mutual tolerance being confined to within the tribe. What is now dignified and cherished as national identity is really little more than functional tribalism reinforced by sundry cultural or learned influences, which are passed from generation to generation as matters of national pride. Whatever its degrees of sophistication, however, nationalism remains realistic in its modus operandi, and tribalism remains rooted in the instinct for survival, and the benefits of collaboration to that end. Considered in this way, it is not surprising that the intertribal tolerance that we are pleased to describe as civilisation is the thinnest of veneers, and can be readily set aside when tribal survival is threatened. The threat may be either a food shortage per se, or aggression by a neighbouring tribe that is facing a food shortage.

Whereas in the animal kingdom generally group aggression is almost entirely related to territory, food and mating rights, as is most individual aggression, the enlarged human perception of the necessities of life have added to the reasons why tribes engage in conflict with other tribes. The substantial necessities which must be gained or defended now include access to the fossil fuels, and other employable minerals which are unevenly distributed in the Earth's crust. To these can be added the urge for power over others, and the acquired belief that the only true godhead is that which the tribe have been indoctrinated into believing in and obeying. A tribal deity with an authoritarian priesthood serves to strengthen common tribal support, for whatever the high priest declares to be the will of the tribal deity. The tribe – en masse – will accept, or be compelled to accept it. Ultimately, however, the seeking of power over neighbours, and the acquisition of their land, or the need for defence against such threats, remains strongly linked to the acquisition and/or retention of life's basic needs – food, water, and mating prospects, but with the addition of the secondary needs such as the materials and fuels which lifestyles now demand.

It is no use debating the morality of this self-interest in either personal or tribal survival. That is how we are programmed to behave. It is an animal inheritance essential to the individual in a natural environment, and essential to the processes of evolution. Since every tribe will tend to multiply to beyond the extent that its food supply can support, there will always be the need for tribes to extend their food-producing territories if that is possible. If a neighbouring tribe is weak, its land is likely to be taken over by a stronger tribe. The need for aggression and the need to defend against aggression are basic conditions of existence, and have played essential roles in the evolutionary progression of Homo sapiens. Cultural efforts to suppress the instinct to survive by whatever means the circumstances make necessary are seldom, if ever, persuasive enough to extinguish that inheritance. It is easy to feel animosity towards other tribes when they are competitors for space and food supplies, and this animosity readily turns into aggressive conflict whenever population pressures cause the available food supply to become insufficient for a tribe.

This animosity is reinforced when languages or even dialects differ. A superficial linguistic difference can show that they are 'not us', while repeated legends of past belligerent contacts will reinforce the prejudice and sense of hostility. These traditional animosities between groups of differing ethnicity and/or language and/or creed, are reinforced by the propaganda of priests, teachers and rulers. Even when there is no need to quarrel over land rights and food, propaganda may be used to sustain a sense of hostility towards another tribe. When the intertribal tension is being caused by, or is strongly influenced by, differing notions of a deity, and duty to that deity, it is then easy to amplify the willingness to fight by declaring the conflict to be 'a holy war'. That is not to say, however, that the instigators of these reinforcing influences are aware of what they are doing and why they are doing it, in terms of human biology and psychology. One must assume that they truly believe their adherences and pronouncements to be true.

History, which one cynic has said does little more than divide one tribe against another, is largely about competitive struggles between individuals, families and tribes. Whether we are at the top of the economic pecking order, or at the bottom of it, depends to a large extent on successes or failures of ourselves, or our ancestors, in competitive struggles of one sort or another. Tribal conflicts are the largest, the most rewarding and/or the most damaging of these. Now, as progressively more nations are acquiring the ability to exterminate more than just their opponents, it may no longer be a matter of which side in an intertribal conflict wins and which side loses. *All could lose!* Thus the concern now is whether tribal antagonisms, despite their inherited genetic basis, have become too dangerous to be accepted passively as an inheritance with which Homo sapiens is lumbered. Survival, as tribes, and even as a species, may no longer depend on the ability to succeed as the aggressor or as the defender. It may depend on whether tribes can overcome those inherited instincts for aggression in pursuit of immediate self-interest, and act collectively instead. That may be an unrealistic hope, but at least we must now keep intertribal conflicts at as low a key as possible, with the employment only of armouries of limited destructive power.

Land hunger and food hunger, and devotion to different, but often allegedly equally militant, deities, is evident in the tribal history of the Israelites and their neighbours and competitors, as recorded in the earlier (Old Testament) books of the Bible. An example of intra-family competition for grazing land is to be found in the story of Abraham and his nephew, Lot. They grazed their livestock separately, but over the same territory in the Negeb. As the number of livestock increased there was the possibility of a famine being precipitated by overgrazing. Thus the senior man, Abraham, told the junior one, Lot, to find land elsewhere on which to graze his animals. Off went Lot in search. No good grazing lands were vacant, of course, for nature abhors vacuums, and when Lot tried to settle in the well-watered plain of the land of Jordan, the Sodomite tribe, which already grazed its livestock there, soon sent him packing. Lot was forced to seek refuge in arid territory that was unoccupied at that time. Perhaps it had been found unsuitable for grazing, or maybe it was used only seasonally, and was not in use at the time Lot came upon it.

Another side of this particular account of a territorial struggle is the recognition of the other deeply rooted instinct, which is to continue the germ line by any possible means. In the course of the retreat from the Jordan plain, Lot's wife had died. When Lot and his two daughters were forced into desert territory and isolation, the two daughters had no immediate prospect of finding mates and achieving succession. It is related that by guile the daughters induced their father to inseminate them, and thereby to sustain the germ line.

This story really has nothing to do with morality, and everything to do with the instinctive endeavours to survive and to breed. Indeed, the entire story is essentially biological. It was overgrazing which caused Abraham to tell Lot to move on because he knew there was insufficient grazing land for the flocks or herds of them both. It was the socially weaker one of the livestock owners that was compelled to migrate. Lot's attempt to occupy the grazing land from another tribe was doomed to failure because he lacked the strength to invade and displace the incumbents. The 'sexual irregularity' met the need of Lot's daughters to endeavour to reproduce, and so give their germ lines their only chance of survival. Thus the story of Lot is a lesson in the realities of life, and serves to illustrate the instinctive urges that dominate our lives.

An equally biological and more salutary story is that of the fate of the Amalekites when they were attacked by the Israelites. Land, it seems, was needed by the Israelites for an expanding tribal population. According to legend, the tribal deity of that time obligingly sanctioned the ethnic cleansing of the Amalekites so that their grazing lands could be annexed by the Israelites. A man called Saul was put in command of this act of tribal extermination, and he did the thorough job needed for the Israelites to have vacant possession of the erstwhile Amelekite territory. Perhaps through compassion, or perhaps through self-interest lest his turn as loser should come one day, Saul spared the life of King Agag. This failure to comply strictly with the real or imaginary, but convenient, orders of the tribal deity, was said to have angered the deity (Samuel 15), and Samuel was dispatched to complete the grisly job. He duly 'hewed Agag to pieces before the

Lord in Gilgal', and presumably the deity was well pleased that the genocide has been made complete. Whether one considers this sanctioning of genocide to be a factual tribal history or fanciful tribal mythology, it is a clear expression of what can happen when a human population has expanded to beyond the supportable number. More land with vacant possession can be obtained only by force and by the liquidation of the vanquished.

More recent occurrences of tribal and ethnic conflicts have similar basic themes. In his text *Mein Kampf*, Adolf Hitler analysed, in a somewhat jaundiced way, the position in which Germany found itself following its defeat in 1918, and the subsequent Treaty of Versailles. By that treaty, Germany was stripped of its overseas colonial territories, and had the extent of its metropolitan territories reduced. Hitler's detestation of a 'non-Aryan' ethnic minority within the federated German States is evident throughout the text. In retrospect, it can be seen that there was a clear indication that if the National Socialists achieved political power, ethnic cleansing would surely follow. Also evident was Hitler's preoccupation with the need to re-establish a dominant influence of the German State in Europe. Thus he wrote:

> The foreign policy of a People's State must first of all bear in mind the duty of securing the existence of the race which is incorporated in this State. And this must be done by establishing a healthy and natural proportion between the number and growth of the population on the one hand and the extent and resources of the territory they inhabit on the other. That balance must be such that it accords with the vital necessities of the people... What I call a healthy proportion is that in which the support of a people is guaranteed by the resources of its own soil and subsoil.

Hitler went on to say,

> Only a sufficiently large space on this earth can assure the independent existence of a people.

Then he wrote:

> We must take our stand on the principles already mentioned in regard to foreign policy: namely, the necessity of bringing our territorial area into just proportion with the number of our population.

There was the hint in *Mein Kampf* of ethnic cleansing of non-Germanic citizens should Hitler's National Socialist party come to power, but if the underlying motivation was to reduce alien demands upon food supplies, it was not stated as such. Ethnic intolerance seemed to be uppermost in Hitler's mind when he was writing *Mein Kampf*. Since the only other way of balancing a population and its food supplies is to reduce the demand on food and/or to increase the nation's food supplies, it is evident that Hitler's message was an echo of the many tribal histories and tribal mythologies. Because the German population could not exist and grow within the confines of the territory over which it still had sovereignty, Germany would have to expand that domain if possible. Thus, while this thesis of Hitler read as an original and perceptive analysis of Germany's dilemma following the Versailles Treaty, it was the repetition of an ancient and oft repeated recipe for tribal survival. That recipe, put simply, is that if one's tribe needs more food than it has access to, it must try colonising the lands of a neighbouring tribe, first by defeating it, and then by displacing or annihilating it. In that way the aggressors can be fed, and can further increase their numbers. Then, when further expansion becomes necessary, the tribe will be even stronger and more able to overcome all opposition. In German terms, they needed 'Lebensraum'.

There are, of course, many variations on the theme of territorial takeovers necessitated by population pressure and food shortage. One way of ensuring that the population grows sufficiently rapidly to strengthen the defences of the expanded tribal territory is to eliminate only the males of the defeated tribe. The womenfolk still of childbearing age can then be taken into the victorious tribe, for employment as breeders of warriors. That strategy, of course, hastens the time when further territorial expansion will be necessary to feed the swollen army of warriors. Something similar underlies the so-called Rape of the Sabines, which has been a popular theme of painters. The Sabines were an ancient Italian tribe in the mountains beyond the Tiber and were conquered by the Romans. The women who were young enough to serve the Romans' need for more womenfolk were taken and incorporated into Roman domestic arrangements.

Whereas the acquisition of neighbouring territories has been the favoured solution to the chronically recurring problem of populations growing to and slightly beyond the sustainable density, this is not always possible. The equality of tribal strengths may discourage the attempt to expand. So might physical barriers such as mountain ranges or deserts. The only possible alternative to starvation and the pestilence that accompanies starvation, when territorial expansion is not possible, might then be to endeavour to keep the population at the supportable level by fair means or foul. Not surprisingly, then, when there is a coexisting ethnic or tribal minority with which a territory is shared, the dominant tribe might seek to solve problem of keeping the population and its food supply in balance by exiling or eliminating the minority faction. Since ethnic and tribal loyalties are strong and deeply rooted, antagonism towards minorities can be easily engineered, especially when the minority embraces a different mythology, or has a distinctly different appearance.

All histories are full of examples of intra- or intertribal cleansing, and none of us is historically innocent of such involvement. The clearances of the native occupants of the colonised territories of Australasia and the Americas were not even done because the land was needed to feed the newcomers. There were markets in Europe for the produce of the new-found lands, and it was largely this market force that made the expulsion of the natives from their lands inevitable. Personal greed and cultural or ethnic antagonisms, however, were other motivations. The resentment and resistance by those being dispossessed was excuse enough for the acts of genocide that occurred. Nearer to home the English invaders/settlers in Ireland banished Irish farming communities from the best agricultural land, compelling them to settle in those unwanted areas where only barely subsistence farming was possible. The heartless banishment of crofters from the Scottish Highlands by the landowners was for no purpose other than to provide sport for the 'gentry'.

This primitive human behaviour still features in contemporary history. Recently the collapse of imposed intertribal cohesion in the Balkan states has seen the upsurge of historical and theological antagonism, carried through to attempts at ethnic cleansing in regions of coexistence of communities of differing ethnicities and theologies. In Rwanda, the hatred between two coexisting tribes recently erupted into another example of intertribal mega-genocide. At least one contemporary observer reported that the fundamental reason for the eruption into civil war in Rwanda was land hunger. It was said, that there were some 6 million inhabitants, but food enough for only 5 million. That would be cause enough for activating the time-honoured genocidal resolution of the population problem.

When there is no scope for territorial expansion, and no disposable minority living within the tribal territory, there is only the one way to limit the risk of famine, the pangs of starvation, and a population crash. That is to keep the population at the supportable density either by controlling the birth rate, or by a practice of post-natal infanticide. Again, the strategies for population limitation by one or other of these means are variable, and are scattered through history. East of Central Europe, the nomadic grazing tribes were often too dispersed and incohesive to be able to expand their territories by force as their numbers increased. Thus population control was imperative for stability, and infanticide was, and perhaps still is, a common and accepted means of preventing numbers from exceeding supportability, in some communities. Such culling of 'surplus progeny' can be gender specific, depending on the relative need of males or females in the circumstances of a particular lifestyle. As was mentioned in Chapter One at least two ancient societies, one in China and the other in Egypt, used sperm barriers or spermicides during sexual intercourse to control pregnancy.

This tribal antagonism, which has often led to belligerency and mass slaughter, might seem to be an unfortunate 'design fault' which spoils the prospect of peaceful coexistence. That, and the will to reproduce beyond survivability, are now destabilising aspects of our natures that we could well do without. Homo sapiens, however, evolved into what it now is, with this relentless intertribal competition for the land needed to feed their numbers, as a crucial determinant of survival of the individual and the evolution of the species. Biological evolution is utterly dependent upon the production and germination of seed greatly in excess of number of progeny that could be adequately fed and survive to maturity. With what are often quite minor variations in the phenotypic expression of the genotypes, those individuals best fitted for any particular set of environmental circumstances are the ones most likely to survive, mature and reproduce. The progenitors of succeeding generations are those that succeed in the competitive struggle for survival, which includes that of gaining and keeping the territory needed for food. It is manifestly evident that aggression in the pursuit of self-interest is a crucial aspect of natural selection. In the natural environments in which the evolution of Homo sapiens occurred there would have been no future for those more passive individuals that were unwilling to compete successfully. Likewise with the pack formation, which serves to enhance the prospects of individual survival. No doubt tribal cohesion also evolved on the basis of collective success and survival selection in consequence.

A major problem that we face now is that we are the products of aeons of the genetic selection of the ability to look after ourselves both individually and tribally, and at anyone else's expense when that is necessary. There can be no genetic selection by which the human genome could have lost its components that determine this behaviour pattern, because that could only occur if the selection was for passiveness, such that the strongest fail and the weakest survive. Likewise, there could be no selection against the tendency to reproduce to excess, so Homo sapiens will always breed to beyond the possibility of the survival of all the progeny unless there is culturally imposed restraint upon reproduction. Only when it is generally understood that *the natural tendency to reproduce in excess of survivability is the basic cause of tribal conflict*, and is the major source of human misery, will we be able to agree upon population limitations and cease to quarrel over the control of the land from which food is obtained.

Such understanding is the imperative axis upon which the

course of human behaviour can be redirected for the common good. The genetic inheritances of the instincts of self-preservation and genetic spreading cannot be changed, but their expressions can be modified by the influences of reason and resultant social pressures. That is how good laws come about, and come to be accepted by most of us. Maybe we do not like curbs on our freedom to be what we are. Most of us understand, however, that the restraints of law create the prospects of living with our neighbours at peace, rather than at war. Whether, as tribes, we can live together at peace rather than at war, depends upon the extent to which we can accept the restraints of a pan-tribal system of law. If such an enforceable legal framework could be used to keep world population within the limits of feedability our futures – even our very future as a species – would then be more secure than it is now. Without it, our uncontrolled genetic inheritances could have disastrous consequences.

Chapter Six

ENVIRONMENTAL POLLUTION

I have no recollection of concern being expressed, more than fifty years ago, about the possibility of environmental damage if the human populations and their activities continued to increase. That was before we had seen the claustrophobic pictures of our little planet taken from outer space, and before we could yet fly halfway round the world in half a day. It was then all but inconceivable that the disturbances wrought and debris dumped by mankind could become a threat to our own well-being.

The advancement of Earth sciences consists of the understanding of the material nature of the Earth and all that is on it, and of the forces which operate both on it and within it. The pace of these advances quickened during the last two to three centuries, and this has provided mankind with the ability to exploit the Earth's substances and to control its forces for the intended betterment of human existence. That increasing mastery over the various components of nature would not have led to the present spectre of threatening consequences were it not for the accompanying upward progression of the sizes of human populations. This was the inevitable result of agricultural progress, for every rise in food production facilitates a population rise. Progress in medicine and public health, by extending the mean longevity of wealthier populations, gave added incentive to the advancement of agriculture, and so to the increases in the rates of population growth.

Thus it is largely because of these two interacting applications of science, first to agriculture, and then to medicine, that the total human population has risen from less than one billion to more than six billion in the course of the last two hundred years. Without this search for an understanding of the context of life, and of the planet on which it has occurred, these applications would not have been, and human life would have remained as brief and brutal as it is for animals generally in their natural environments. With human nature being fundamentally that of animals generally, intense competition between individuals, families and tribes, would have been the way of deciding who lived into and through adulthood, and who died prematurely. The premature deaths would have been the way by which populations were kept more or less matched to their food supplies.

For long there was no good reason for seeing anything other than goodness in the advancements of both agriculture and medicine. And for long there seemed to be no reason for concern about the extent to which mankind was disturbing and exploiting everything in and on the Earth that could be put to use. With the vastness of the land, the oceans and the atmosphere, it was all but inconceivable that these human activities could cause any significant interference with the natural orders of things. Nor did it seem likely that the disposal of the waste products of humans and of human activities could be sufficient to disrupt those orders, or ecosystems. This complacency was naive, but not entirely so, because the interacting components of ecosystems provide buffers by which minor disturbances are without long-term consequences. The extent to which the human population has expanded is the principal reason for the environmental damage that has been done, and is now being done. The damage caused by numbers alone has been compounded by the increasingly extravagant complexity of many lifestyles. Ever greater perceived needs for happiness compels ever greater exploitation of the Earth's natural resource, and ever more waste material to be disposed of somewhere in the environment. Over the last 200 years the increases in environmental disturbance caused by human activity has been considerably more than the sixfold increase in human numbers.

As was stated in Chapter One, it is now more than fifty years since concern was first being expressed about the implication of the recent revolutionary progress in the medical sciences. Lives 'saved' (meaning 'prolonged') by medical interventions would be prolonged only transiently unless there was a sufficient concurrent rise in food production to sustain a progressively increasing world population. The concern, then, when the life-saving capabilities of medicine leaped forward was whether there could be a matching agricultural revolution of sufficient magnitude to effect the prolongation of the saved lives. If that could be achieved, it would not only have to be sustainable indefinitely thereafter, but also to be continuously increased thereafter. More adults mean more children. In the fullness of time this leads to more mated couples and even more children. Unless somehow the brake could be applied, there would thus be a geometric rise in population. Short of deliberate human restraint, the only braking there could be would be the calamities of hunger, disease and war, collectively describable as a population crash.

There were historical warnings of disastrous consequences if the soil were to be over-exploited in the bid to sustain the needed level of food production for an increasing human population. The extent to which the collapse of the wheat harvest in North Africa, needed to feed the Romans and their far-flung armies, is attributable to a natural climatic change, or was brought about by the over-exploitation of the soil, remains debatable. Whatever the cause, the crop failure contributed substantially to the fall of the Roman Empire. The collapse of soil structure and soil fertility of land in the Midwest territories of the United States earlier in the twentieth century, however, was still fresh in our minds fifty years ago. Land upon which corn was grown year after year had become organically exhausted and turned to dust. This was then blown away, leaving behind infertile 'bad lands'.

The danger of a recurrence has not passed, for while inorganic mineral applications to the soil can satisfy the minerals needed for plant growth, they do not sustain the structure of the soil needed to retain the moisture. For that, reliance is upon the ploughing in of the plant and animal residues, though this alone would not be sufficient for the preservation of the soil structure indefinitely, and particularly if ever higher crop yields are sought. What can befall a human population when crop failure occurs on a massive scale, whether caused naturally or by human activities, is exemplified by the recently reported evidence that the abrupt disappearance of the Mayan civilisation some 1,200 years ago, in what is now Southern Mexico and Guatemala, was due to drought and crop failures when the rains failed.

There is little that mankind can do to prevent the consequences of climatic changes which are wholly unrelated to human activities, but one can anticipate such occurrences, and be prepared for them, as were the early Egyptians. By controlling population so that not all of each year's harvest was consumed in that year, some of the harvest could be saved to buffer the community against the consequences of a bad harvest. We could, if we were collectively wise enough, and sufficiently collaborative, take steps to minimise the extent of climatic changes contributed to by human activity, and thereby minimise the consequences of such changes. For that, we must be collectively appreciative of the effects our increasing numbers and increasingly extravagant lifestyles are having upon the ecosystems of which we are part, and upon which we depend. We must then cease to deny the reality of atmospheric pollution; of man-induced climate changes; of reduced and contaminated aquifers; of the collapse of over-harvested oceanic fish populations; of the reckless destruction of forests, and of the exhaustion and/or contamination of arable farmland. And we must cease to believe that the only thing that matters both at present and in the future is economic growth and the creation of wealth, regardless of what harmful effects this will have upon our inheritors of the Earth.

There is a spreading awareness of all these adverse consequences of the activities now necessary to feed and support the often-extravagant lifestyles of the greatly expanded human population. Unfortunately it is highly unlikely that the awareness will become general enough for drastic corrective action to be taken, or for mankind's collective concern for the future to compete successfully with the prime concern for the quality of contemporary life. Our genetic inheritance puts self first – and self first means this generation, and perhaps the next generation, but no further into the future. Thus the instinct for self and personal survival will almost certainly continue to be the overriding determinant of our behaviour. That is the Achilles heel of democracy, which is largely seen as the best means of protecting peoples against tyrants. Invariably the popular vote is not for what is in the best long-term interest of mankind in general, but for what is deemed to be in the best interest of the individual voter at the present time. Nobody votes for the future if it spoils the present.

From the industrial revolution onwards the accoutrements of individual lifestyles and of the wider fabric of societies have grown ever more complex, and have become extended to ever more peoples and societies. All those not yet enjoying 'the good life' are now longing to do so. We should have realised that there was the risk of massive environmental pollution long before the evidence for it became apparent.

Only some twenty-five years ago did the first warnings occur of the likelihood that with the increasing impacts of increasing numbers of humans and human activities, we were polluting our environment massively, and possibly irreversibly. These warnings were either wholly ignored, or dismissed as the scare-mongering products of misdirected imaginations. It would be foolish now to ignore the warnings. There is simply too much evidence of global environmental pollution to allow it to be dismissed because of the economic and social inconvenience of attempting to reverse the trend. An unwillingness to act appropriately and adequately to avert the risk of man-made disasters could have three possible explanations.

One reason for this unwillingness to act appropriately and sufficiently is the still persisting illusion of the vastness of the seas, the atmosphere, and the land. It is, of course, impossible for the demands and the waste products of any one of us to so disturb the environment as to spoil things for future generations. The activities of a human population of six thousand million, however, are now causing a very substantial degree of pollution. This is a macro-scale version of the public swimming bath illusion: when one small addition of nitrogenous matter is made to so much water it is diluted into insignificance, but when a great number of such antisocial indiscretions occur in any one day, the additions become readily detectable. In well-used public swimming baths continuous corrective treatment of the water is necessary to avoid possible harmful consequences. A quotation that caught my eye recently neatly expresses this cumulative effect of a great many individuals: 'No snowflake in an avalanche feels responsible' (attributed to Stanislav J Lec).

Another possible reason for the unwillingness of much of mankind to face up to the reality of what we are doing to our planet, and to the ecosystems of which we are part, and upon which we depend for our continued existence, is the belief of many that Homo sapiens was specially created, and that the protection of the Creator can be relied upon to rescue us from our own follies. Even the most devout 'supernaturalists' must surely agree that instances of a divine intervention into the affairs of mankind, if they ever truly occur, are exceeding rare. Furthermore, there is a bizarrely incomprehensible selectivity in what is attributed by some to divine intervention. Whatever one elects to believe for one's own comfort, it would surely be prudent to conduct ourselves at least in relation to the finite nature of our environment as if we lack any special supernatural protection, and are responsible to ourselves for what we are doing. Having the exceptional powers of reason and self-determination, whether given or evolved, we can, if we so choose, use those faculties to the best of our ability to spare ourselves from a self-made disaster. Even if, as individuals, we calculate that we can get through our own brief lifetimes before disaster strikes, surely we should remain concerned about the world we will be leaving for our grandchildren, and their grandchildren, to inherit.

A third, and likely, possibility is that mankind, for all its self-congratulatory illusion of intellectual sophistication, cannot free itself from the domination of our inherited instincts. These influences are crucial for the individual to survive for long enough to procreate, and thereby contribute to the evolutionary adaptation of the species to a continuously changing natural environment. These instinctive influences compel the adoption of whatever lifestyle maximises the material success and satisfaction of one's own lifetime, largely regardless of others, and with little or no concern about future generations.

This paramount concern for oneself and one's immediate dependants is evident in everything we do, from our self-promotion in the workplace to how we vote at election times, and how we seek educational advantage for our own progeny, often to the detriment of society at large. An unashamed and careless self-interest is evident in the attitudes of Middle England to both GM foodstuffs and organically produced foodstuffs. In both instances the concern is for personal welfare: GM foods might harm me, and organically grown food might be better for me. What effect the influence of these attitudes might have on human health and welfare elsewhere in the world takes second place, or none at all.

Capitalist-based societies, with their emphasis on competition, economic growth, and wealth creation by successful entrepreneurs, rest four-square upon a primary concern for self. There is no clearer example of this than the refusal of the current (2004) US Administration to contribute to the curbing of carbon dioxide emissions in to the atmosphere and the consequential global warming. To do so, it is feared, would be harmful to the US economy. This might lower the living standards of its citizenship, which might then vote the incumbent President out of office. The President would take the rap from his own people if he acts in a way disadvantageous to them, and from 'the others' for having acted irresponsibly if he did not. The fault, if fault it be, lies with human nature: 'me first' personally, and 'us first' tribally, with survival today being more important to the extant members of the tribe, whatever the consequence will be for others, and for future generations. By contrast, socialist societies have invariably failed because concern for self always wins over concern for others whenever the choice of 'us or them' has to be made. Thus it is the ambitions of most of us, if not all of us, to do as well as we can for ourselves. That inevitably provides the incentive for escalating industrial expansion. Hence the unbridled exploitation of the substances of the Earth's crust as an expanding human population, needs to be fed, and demands all the benefits of contemporary societies. It would seem, then, that these inborn behavioural characteristics of Homo sapiens compel our negative impacts on the environment, and could be suppressed only with great difficulty and resolve.

We can always argue that we are not blameworthy for what we are by nature. That does not necessarily mean that we, like the yeast cells in the brewer's vat, are destined to multiply until we exhaust the food supply or until we poison our environment with our own end products, and suffer an almighty population crash, because we are incapable of doing anything about it. The peculiarity of human awareness by which we can know where we are heading allows us the possibility of choosing another road. The possibility of population control to avert a population crash has already been explored. The possibility of environmental control to avert a population crash is multifaceted, and each of the major environmental injuries referred to earlier in this chapter could, if we had the will to do so, be addressed and reduced. To be successful in averting the major human tragedies resulting from a destabilised environment, corrections must be effected by the combined resolve of humanity at large, for piecemeal therapy by minorities of us cannot stem the rot.

The instinctive prime concern with our own lifetimes and our own prosperity, makes such a massive endeavour to reset the course of human destiny, a difficult medicine to prescribe. Only by a worldwide understanding that we will not be able to increase our numbers and desecrate our environment for ever, or even for much longer, can there be any hope of a sufficiently determined remedy being adopted.

No doubt it will be argued by those who want to follow a policy of 'business as usual' that the elevated living standards and qualities of life that many of us now enjoy rest upon capitalism, and that capitalism can only prosper while there is continuous economic growth. If that means that the wheels of industry must now spin ever faster, because nobody wants to stop them, nor knows how to stop them, then the sandwich board man advising us to prepare to meet our doom will be proved right, though for a different reason from that supposed by him. It will be because we failed to tame our natural instincts. The land, the oceans and the atmosphere, can only accommodate so much of the detritus of humans; their industries and their pastimes, before the buffering capacity of ecosystems are exhausted. Changes in the ecosystems must then occur in ways that may be incompatible with the continued supremacy of the organisms that has caused the changes.

The dilemma in which the 6,000 million human aspirants to the 'good time' are now placed is that the still rising world population; the rising levels of pollution of land, sea and air; the rising sea levels, the changing climates, the depletion and poisoning of aquifers, and the excessive demands being made upon arable farming, are being down-played because any attempt to reduce either population growth or pollution growth could have unwelcome economic, social and political consequences for the present human incumbents. This greater concern for today than for tomorrow stays the hands of governments, and especially democratic governments. Any governmental attempt to curb individual procreative liberty, and/or to curb environmental pollution, by restraining industrial activities and lifestyles, would be a recipe for electoral defeat which would end any well-intended endeavour to protect the future.

Far from any serious and adequate degree of restraint, the 'Western' economics and lifestyles are now expanding to encompass the newer industrially successful nations across the world; to boost world trade, and to sustain the economic growth upon which the buoyancy of 'Western-style' nations depend to avoid depression. This non-retrenchment is not entirely in pursuit of commercial advancement, but also because it is the only way to keep a now massive workforce employed, and to sustain its living standards. It is not surprising, then, that industrialists and the political institution that they support are acting in tandem to persuade electorates that any cutback in industrial exploitation of the Earth's crust to conserve the environment for future generations is unnecessary and would damage nations and homesteads alike. The citizens of the United States of America were assured by their incumbent political leader, upon his taking office, that nothing would be done by him that could harm the economic well-being of the citizenship. That was what the 'captains' of industry wanted and expected to hear him say, as did much of the electorate as well. This priority of 'self and now' is, as is laboured in this text, a completely natural expression of a dominant instinct. Survival in all animal species is an intensely egocentric endeavour, which may extend to one's own progeny, but seldom much further. If, with all our latent ability to reason and direct our lives less selfishly, we are unable to overcome our servitude to genetic command, we must consider the possibility that we are unable to rescue ourselves from ultimate self- destruction.

With the sustained inflow of energy from the sun, this little orbiting planet that we share as home is not the strict equivalent of the more nearly closed system of the brewer's vat. With this continuous energy input, and the evolved potential of the human central nervous system and consciousness, we could endeavour together to postpone the ultimate disaster of an organism which is well adapted to a prevailing set of environmental circumstances, but is evidently unable or unwilling to adapt to change when its environment becomes changed. If the Earth's dominant species cannot adapt to the environmental changes brought about by that species own activities, it may ultimately fail, and be replaced by some other life form.

Chapter Seven

THE HYDROCARBONS, THE ATMOSPHERE AND LIFE

Life: Its Beginning, the Human Present and the Human Future

How life first came to be on Earth remains largely speculative, but its genesis must have occurred well before the emergence of organisms capable of photosynthesis. Before that, organisms could not trap and utilise solar energy and must have obtained the energy to sustain life, and to reproduce themselves, by breaking down (katabolising) molecular structures on or in the Earth's crust into simpler molecules of lower energy content. Such energy sources were finite, of course, and had life remained dependent upon this earth-bound energy supply, these 'fuels' would eventually have become exhausted, and life would have ceased at an early stage in its evolution. There would then have been no knowledge of it, for the one species that has the evolved ability to seek an understanding of the causation of life would never have come to be.

With the evolution of organisms that could convert solar energy into the energy-rich chemical components of their body tissues, the possibility that life forms would exhaust the energy supply, and thereby become extinct, was over. It is self-evident that throughout the aeons it has taken for life to evolve from a small reproductive 'blob' into the vast array of life forms that now exist, there were always some life forms that were able to remain compatible with continuously occurring environment changes, while many others failed to do so and became extinct. All extant life forms are more or less compatible with present geophysical and other environmental circumstances that constitute their particular habitats, but not all extant species will be able to survive future environmental changes. Only those able to adapt to those changes will do so, while others will fail. Indeed, the changes in environments now resulting from human activities are causing many species to become extinct. Mankind should not assume, therefore, that it can do what it likes to itself and to its environment without endangering itself.

When photosynthesising organisms first evolved, the Earth's atmosphere had a much higher content of carbon dioxide and much lower content of oxygen than it has now. It is believed that an early photosynthetic life form, somewhat akin to blue-green algae of today, developed into a thick carpet across the oceanic expanses of water. This proliferation was, presumably, at a sufficient depth below the surface to avoid destruction by the damaging effects of a high level of ultraviolet radiation from the sun, and the high surface temperature of the water at that time.

The biological photosynthesis of organic matter involves a complexity of processes that need not be considered here. The relevant consideration is that the solar energy is trapped by light-sensitive molecular structures and used to synthesise energy-rich sugar molecules $n(C_6H_{12}O_6)$, where n is the number of simple sugar units bonded together to yield more complex sugar-based biomolecules: the starches, celluloses and lignins. The basic equation which describes this photosynthesis of sugars is:

Water + carbon dioxide + solar energy, is built (anabolised) into a basic sugar molecule, with the release of oxygen, or

$$6H_2O + 6CO_2 + \text{Energy} = C_6H_{12}O_6 + 6O_2 \qquad (1)$$

Thus carbon dioxide is taken up from the atmosphere and oxygen is expelled into it. If, upon its death, the tissue of a photosynthesising organism is totally broken down (katabolised) the equation is reversed, by various, and sometimes very complex, routes:

$$C_6H_{12}O_6 + 6O_2 = 6H_2O + 6CO_2 + \text{liberated energy} \quad (2)$$

Oxygen is then taken back from the atmosphere, and carbon dioxide is released back into it.

The atmospheric gases are then as before, and the temporarily stored energy, of solar origin, will have been liberated as heat, which then flows down a thermal gradient to entropy[2]. That is what happens when, for example, straw, which is the product of photosynthesis, is burned. When the straw is from a recent harvest, equation (2) follows close upon equation (1), and the concentrations of oxygen and carbon dioxide in the atmosphere are unchanged. If, however, the dead organic matter has no access to oxygen, its organic structure remains intact. Without the reversal of the photosynthetic equation the carbon remains locked up in these organic tissues and the oxygen stays in the atmosphere.

Upon the death of the early photosynthesising organisms which were spread across the oceans, they would have sunk into the oxygen-less depth of the oceans. The carbon derived from atmospheric carbon dioxide, and the hydrogen derived from water, together with the energy derived from the sun, are then kept in chemical bondage. For so long as there is no access to oxygen, the chemistry will stay that way, and in consequence the atmosphere will become progressively richer in oxygen and poorer in carbon dioxide.

---

[2] Energy, when free to do so, will flow down an energy gradient to a lower level. If the gradient is of sufficient magnitude and the energy flow is of sufficient force, the flow can be used to do work as it moves from a higher level to a lower one. Entropy, as used in this text, is descriptive of the lowest attainable energy level from which no further downward energy flow can occur. Most of the energy emitted by the sun flows directly to that lowest level where it must stay thereafter in a state of total disorganisation, or chaos. A very small fraction of the total solar radiated energy impinges upon a planetary surface, and is temporarily halted and raises the temperature of the planetary surface. Planet Earth, with its atmosphere, oceans and the complex high-energy molecules of living systems, may retain that energy at a level above that of entropy for very considerable lengths of time, partly as thermal energy, but particularly as the chemical energy of living things. In various circumstances, however, some naturally occurring, and some due to deliberate human activity, that retained chemical energy is released, and is free to complete the flow to entropy. Some of the atomic energy of radioactive components of the substance of the Earth, when spontaneously emitted, likewise then flows to entropy. This spontaneous release of energy from radioactive material can be harnessed and directed to do work as it moves down an energy gradient.

Evidently, unreversed photosynthetic activity occurred on a sufficiently massive scale to raise the oxygen content of the atmosphere to more or less what it is now – about 21%, and to reduce the atmospheric carbon dioxide content to the very low level of about 0.04%. Such a large and sustained change in the composition of the atmosphere indicates that somewhere beneath the Earth's terrestrial and aqueous surfaces there is a great mass of unoxidised organic matter. Over time this sunken vegetable debris has undergone some degree of chemical change – from carbohydrate-rich material (compounds of carbon, hydrogen and oxygen) to hydrocarbon-based material (compounds of carbon and hydrogen). This change renders the fossilised organic debris more readily combustible if or when it is brought into contact with the oxygen-rich atmosphere, and is raised to a high enough temperature for the oxidative reaction to occur rapidly. Thus when these hydrocarbon deposits are found, and are brought to the surface as crude oil and natural gas, they readily oxidise, or burn, and in doing so, give up the energy captured from the sun aeons earlier. Thus the hydrocarbon materials (oil, natural gas and coal) extracted from beneath the land and oceans are called fossil fuels.

It is possible that not all the subterranean hydrocarbon deposits derived from the partial catabolism of the carbohydrate structures of dead plants. Petroleum geologists believe that heat and pressure deep underground could have produced some of the hydrocarbons from carbon and water. There is no agreement on this possibility, and in a comment on a recent assertion that all hydrocarbons were formed in this way (*New Scientist*, 17 August 2002, p.17), it is stated that this shows reckless disregard for the disciplines of organic chemistry and for decades of research. It may or may not be significant that the protagonists of this non-biological origin of the hydrocarbon deposits are in the oil exploration industry. This industry has a vested commercial interest in any evidence or point of view which might be used to absolve the fossil fuel industry from any responsibility for global warming.

All the evolution of life that has occurred since the occurrence of this massive photosynthetic bonanza has occurred beneath this 'new' biologically created atmosphere, and has been greatly influenced by it. Much of life, therefore, is now dependent upon the composition of the atmosphere staying very much as it is. Obviously, then, the bulk of the deposits of hydrocarbons need to stay right where they are, hidden beneath the Earth's terrestrial and aquatic surfaces, and well away from the atmospheric oxygen, so that the reversion of the hydrocarbon compounds to water and carbon dioxide cannot occur.

The discovery, extraction and combustion of just enough of these hydrocarbon deposits to provide the modest domestic needs and comforts of a much smaller world population would have been relatively harmless, since the extensive forests and the oceans can both take up at least some of the liberated carbon dioxide. The use of coal, another hydrocarbon complex derived from incompletely decomposed plant material, as an energy source, however, greatly contributed to the progression of the industrial revolution. It replaced wood, the continued dependency upon which, as a fuel for industry, would have led to an even earlier ecological disaster. The abundance of the European coal deposits greatly aided the growth of industrialisation and the accompanying rapid rise in human numbers. The discovery and exploitation of oil deposits later replaced coal as the principal energy source upon which industries depend. There is now increasing use of the gaseous hydrocarbons, partly because they are there, and partly because the combustion of these gaseous hydrocarbons is marginally less damaging to the atmosphere than is fossil oil or coal. The now vastly inflated mass of humanity is dedicated to the continuing expansion of industrialisation, for that is on what the somewhat artificial, but gladly accepted, qualities of contemporary lives of many of us now depend. Consequently humanity remains heavily dependent on the fossil fuels for the energy requirements of industries and modern lifestyles, even though the dangers of doing so are becoming generally acknowledged.

The emission of carbon dioxide into the atmosphere resulting from the combustion of fossil fuels is currently estimated to exceed 6,000 million tonnes per annum. That is a familiar figure, for it amounts to the emission of one metric tonne of carbon dioxide each year for each human being on Earth. As with the world's food supplies, however, the fossil fuel usage is not equitably distributed. Data for 1994 (Flavin and Tunali, 1996) shows that in 1994 the USA was the biggest fossil fuel burner with the emission into the atmosphere of more than 5 tonnes per person per annum. In the United Kingdom this figure was less than 3 tonnes per year per person, and in India it was only 0.25 tonnes per year per person. In the United States domestic air conditioning and immodest means of personal vehicular transport add substantially to the industrial dependence upon fossil fuels. So does its agriculture, so it should be noted in partial mitigation that United States agriculture supplies the tables of many other peoples, as well as its own overweight citizenship.

Despite the almost unrelenting effort of the fossil fuel consortia to find, extract and market these hydrocarbon deposits, there are, as yet, no reports of a measurable decline in the oxygen content of the atmosphere. The progressive rise in atmospheric carbon dioxide content of the atmosphere, which is almost certainly largely attributable to the burning of fossil fuels, is still nowhere near enough to have any direct adverse effect on human bodily functions or, indeed, on those of animal life generally. On that score, then, there is no need for immediate alarm over the wanton use of hydrocarbon substances as fuels. A study by the UK Meteorological Office (see *New Scientist,* 30 October 1999, p.5), however, has indicated that if carbon dioxide emissions remain unchecked many of the world's forests will be killed by the end of the next century. That same report indicates that it is already too late to halt a progressive rise in the sea level over the next hundred years. This could be of the order of two metres or more, even if the combustion of hydrocarbons were now to be reduced to the extent that there is no further rise in the level of atmospheric carbon dioxide.

Global Temperature and What Can Change It

Any inert mass, when exposed to and absorbing an energy flow, will warm up. When the inert mass is a barren waterless planet without an atmosphere, the surface facing the sun is intercepting the emission of short-wave (high energy) solar radiation, which warms the planet surface. When, with the planet's rotation, this warmed surface no longer faces the sun, the recently gained heat flows away to the cold night sky by long-wave (low energy) radiation. The cycle of warming and cooling, as the planet surface faces away from the sun, is much more complicated and more quantitatively variable when the planet is the Earth. This is largely because it has a gaseous atmosphere and the sub-atmospheric surface is partly solid land and partly liquid water. Water has a much higher specific heat than land has. This and the continuous mixing of surface water with deeper water, causes the oceans to warm up more slowly than solid land does during the periods of solar exposure. The aqueous surfaces also lose heat more slowly during exposure to the cold night sky. Furthermore, the evaporation of water during exposure to sunshine, aided by air movement, gives rise to cloud formation, and adds gasified water (vapour) to the atmosphere. Air movement (wind), largely due to convection as warmed air rises about heated surfaces, and resultant differences in atmospheric pressure, contribute to the variable environmental condition which we call weather. Climate, with its seasonal changes, is largely the consequence of the tilt of the Earth's axis relative to the sun. Climates and seasons are more predicable, at least within the span of a human lifetime, but are not wholly invariable. Changes in climate do occur; sometimes it would seem, cyclically over lengthy time periods, as with the ice ages. Some of these may relate to variations in solar activities. When considering the causation of the global warming that is now evident, such spontaneous occurrences obviously need to be considered.

The mixture of gases which constitute atmospheric air (mostly nitrogen, with some 21% oxygen, a much smaller concentration of carbon dioxide, and even smaller concentrations of other gases) reduces the amount of solar radiation reaching the solid and aqueous surfaces. The natural atmospheric variables are the water vapour content, and the variable cloud cover. Some of the solar radiation is reflected by the atmosphere, and this includes much of the high energy ultraviolet wavelength radiation. Only a variable proportion of the total solar radiation intercepted by planet Earth, therefore, reaches the Earth's solid and aqueous surfaces.

The atmosphere also impedes the long-wave (low energy) radiation from the Earth's surfaces, especially to the much colder sky. This loss of heat by long wavelength radiation is most noticeable at night because there is no counterbalancing incoming short wavelength solar radiation. The atmospheric resistance to the outward long-wave radiation is greater than the atmospheric resistance to the inward solar radiation, and it is the differential between energy inflow and energy outflow that produces surface warming. It is this phenomenon that is analogously referred to as the *greenhouse effect*. The glass panes of a greenhouse similarly impede long-wave outward radiation more so than the inward short-wave solar radiation, with the resultant heat retention within the greenhouse. This simile derives from a theoretical consideration of the surface temperature of the Earth by Fourier (1824), who likened the atmosphere, which consists of invisible gases and clouds, to a giant glass dome. A *greenhouse gas* is one that, as a constituent of the atmosphere, is a substantial contributor to this heat retention at the Earth's terrestrial and oceanic surfaces. When a change in the atmospheric concentration of one of these gases occurs, there could be a detectable change in the balance energy inflow and energy outflow, and thereby a detectable change in the mean surface temperature of the Earth.

Arrhenius (1896) recognised that carbon dioxide, although only a minor component of atmospheric air, is a significant contributor to the greenhouse effect. He pointed out that if human activities should cause an increase in atmospheric carbon dioxide, global warming could occur. At that time it seemed unlikely that the extent of human activities would be sufficient to cause a detectable and significant increase in mean global surface temperature. Since then, however, the burning of fossilised organic debris has increased enormously. In the last half of the twentieth century there was a more than fourfold increase in the combustion of hydrocarbons (Fig. 7.1A) Six billion tonnes has already been cited as the amount of carbon dioxide now released into the atmosphere every year. At the same time the rate of destruction of forests, which take up carbon dioxide from the atmosphere, has also greatly increased.

Another greenhouse gas that is released naturally into the atmosphere from marshlands and elsewhere is methane. Human activities are also augmenting its release. This is from mining operations; the now much extended rice paddies needed to feed increasing populations and the eructations (belches) of domesticated ruminants animals, the numbers of which have likewise been greatly increased to meet the demand for meat and dairy produce by a rapidly increasing human population. The sum of these atmospheric perturbations resulting from human activities could be contributing substantially, and perhaps principally, to the global warming which coincides with the intensification of these human activities.

It is clear, however, that irrespective of the possible perturbation to the atmosphere attributable to human activities, climate and weather are the consequences of a complex set of interacting physical circumstances, some of which are not fixed natural circumstances, but change on both short and extended timescales. There must be changes in the geophysics of the planet to have caused such periodic occurrences as the ice ages. Major disturbances by earthquakes and volcanic eruptions have also caused planet-wide environmental changes. Furthermore, there are variations in the intensities of extraterrestrial occurrences, such as the sun spots and other cosmic radiations, which may have both minor and major effects on our planetary climate. This complexity of regular and irregular contributors to climate surely means that the approximate predictability of the climate and weather changes experienced in a lifetime cannot be taken as fixed 'norms'. There have been big variations in the past, and changes unrelated to human activities could be occurring now.

While there can now be little doubt that the mean surface temperature of the planet Earth is increasing, opinions are divided as to its cause. It could be a naturally occurring event over which humans are exerting no influence and over which humans can exercise no control. It could be, to some extent at least, the consequence of an increase in the greenhouse effect of the atmosphere caused by human activity.

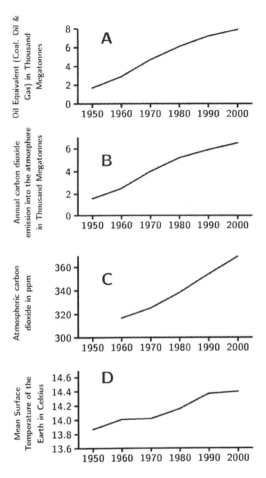

FIG. 7.0   SMOOTHED GRAPHS BASED ON MORE DETAILED GRAPHS GIVEN IN
VITAL SIGNS 2002 & 2003 OF CHANGES DURING THE SECOND HALF
OF THE TWENTIETH CENTURY IN A) THE ANNUAL AMOUNT OF
FOSSIL FUELS USED; B) THE ANNUAL AMOUNT OF CARBON DIOXIDE
LIBERATED   INTO   THE   ATMOSPHERE;   C)   THE   CHANGING
CONCENTRATION OF CARBON DIOXIDE IN THE ATMOSPHERE, AND
D) CHANGES IN THE MEAN ANNUAL TEMPERATURE OF THE EARTH'S
SURFACE.

It has been stated from time to time, and for one reason or another, that in the course of the last few centuries there have been fluctuations in surface temperature as great, or greater, than those now occurring. This is taken by some as reason to doubt a human involvement in the current rise, and to postpone any change in human activities which may slow, halt or even reverse the rise. There is, however, no solid evidence to justify this disbelief and delay. On the contrary, researches at the Climate Research Unit at the University of East Anglia have reported (Jones et al., 1999) that mean global temperature has risen to a higher level since 1975 than it was at any time in the previous 500 years. Mann and Jones (2003) and Jones and Mann (2004) have deduced from natural and documentary archives of the past, that the same can be said for the last 2,000 years in the Northern Hemisphere. This is probably also true for the Southern Hemisphere but, for that half of the globe, the archival data is too sparse to be certain. In the absence any alternative hypothetical or demonstrable explanation for this temperature rise, and with clear evidence of a strong correlation between the rise in fossil fuel consumption (Fig. 7.1A), the emission of carbon dioxide into the atmosphere (Fig. 7.1B), the rise in atmospheric carbon dioxide (Fig. 7.1C), and the rise in global temperature (Fig 7.1D), the continuing attempts to absolve mankind from any responsibility are manifestly very thin indeed.

It is estimated that some 55% of the global warming could be the consequence of the increase in atmospheric carbon dioxide, with the remainder attributable to other greenhouse gases, particularly methane, nitrous oxide, and chlorine compounds (CFCs), which are also increasing in the atmosphere because of human activities.

Although a gradual but irreversible rise in mean surface temperature of the Earth by a few degrees Celsius will not be a direct threat to human life per se, it can be expected to have a multitude of indirect effects on human welfare. The rise in sea level due to water expansion as its temperature rises, and to the melting of ice masses, will deprive mankind of low-lying coastal areas of habitation and food production. Dramatic changes in both climate and weather can be expected. Models indicate that some regions will become hotter and others cooler; that some regions will become drier and others wetter, and that the weather of some regions will become more tranquil, while others will become much stormier and more hurricane-prone. Thus local changes in climate and weather may differ greatly, with some of them seemingly inconsistent with a rise in mean global surface temperature.

There will also be many secondary adverse effects, some of which will greatly affect human health and welfare. There will be changes in the geographic distribution of disease-transmitting vectors, which will cause geographic changes in disease patterns, and changes in the extent of lands suitable for habitation, and for food production. These could be the most devastating consequences of global warming, with the reduction in land available for food production and habitation being the most intractable. The consequences will be both per se, and because tribes will have to fight over territorial rights as land threatened with inundation is evacuated, and as food production falls.

The rise in the sea level is a consequence of the melting of the solid water in the polar regions, and in high altitude glaciers elsewhere, coupled to the thermal expansion of oceanic waters close to the surface. As stated earlier, a rise in sea level, even of only half a metre, will deprive many populations living in coast areas of both living space and land for food production. Because populations in many regions of the world are close to that number that the regional food supplies can support, the displaced humans, like Lot, will find little in the way of empty lands above the rising sea level. The displaced populations could then just die of starvation *en masse* or, if their belligerency is sufficient, they may succeed in the conquest of higher land. Then there will be either the annihilation of the defeated inhabitants, or a 'domino effect' sequence of tribal or territorial conflicts until a status quo is achieved. Deaths in battle may well play a substantial role in readjusting population size in relation to the food supply.

There is growing evidence that the general trend of global warming will be much more dramatic and dynamic than earlier models predicted. It is now considered likely that before the end of the twenty-first century, the average global temperature could be between 1.4°C and 5.8°C above what it was at the beginning of the twentieth century. Just what affects this will have regionally, which will differ widely, remains to be resolved, but some indicators of what is happening are quite alarming. The dramatic contrast of the photographs of a glacier close by Huaras (Peru) taken in 1980 and twenty years later (Lynas, 2003) indicate the extent to which ice melt is now occurring. Confirmation of this is the evidence that the ice cover of the Arctic Sea has thinned by some 40% during the past fifty years (see *New Scientist,* 1 November 2003, p.12).

It is still maintained by some (see P Stott, 2003), that the current global warming, which is undoubtedly occurring, is unrelated to human activities, and furthermore, is beyond human ability to do anything to prevent its progression and consequences. The evidence for that interpretation is nowhere near as convincing as is that for human involvement. If, however, it should be proved to be true, and that a reduction in the amount of carbon dioxide now being discharged into the atmosphere will do nothing to stop this, that human absolution would bring no comfort. The consequences are dependent on the occurrence, not upon the cause of the occurrence. Such opinions, however, need to be carefully scrutinised to distinguish between honestly reached interpretations of evidence, and misrepresentations motivated by self-interest. There are powerful lobbies, supported by oil-producers and purveyors, dedicated to the promulgation of any evidence or argument that could be seen to justify the continued massive use of the fossil fuels. In the very same week that Stott (2003) drew attention to recently published indications of the non-involvement of hydrocarbon combustion in global warming, it was reported in *The Observer* (a London Sunday newspaper) that it has obtained documents indicating that the US central administration, which has well-recognised and strong connections to the US oil industry, has ignored or misreported findings of its own researchers which link the burning of hydrocarbons and the current global warming.

Thus, in order to dissociate the rise in temperature now occurring from human activities, there would be need for a natural geophysical explanation for it, and that is distinctly lacking. If, despite all prevailing reason otherwise, it should be true that the current global warming is unrelated to human activities, that could be both good news and bad news. The good news is that we need not rush into using other energy sources, and can continue, for a while at least, with our prodigal lifestyles, careless of the future. The bad news is that if global warming is unstoppable, the current 6,000 million Homo sapiens will quite soon have less land to live on and to grow food on. The result of that, if history tells us anything, is that there will be all manner of unpleasant consequences as we fight each other, ever more desperately, for access to what space and food there is. Thus should this non-involvement in the cause of global warming be confirmed, and it has to be accepted that we can do nothing about it, the need to make every possible humane effort to halt the rise in the human population would be even more urgent than it is already. Contraception is so much kinder than starvation and genocide.

Persuading both people and their governments to escalate the transition from dependence upon fossil fuels to less harmful and more enduring supplies of energy will not be easy. A greatly influential objection to a rapid conversion, particularly in democratically governed nations, is that a fairly abrupt retreat from fossil fuel dependency would slow down the rate of economic growth. This, it is feared, would precipitate an economic slump, in which many would suffer. No government dependent upon popular votes will want to take that road, even if convinced of its necessity. That is because the popular vote goes for what is best for the individual voter here and now. The deliberate risk of an economic slump would not meet that criterion. Governments, therefore, have always to calculate whether a shift in energy source is to the immediate advantage or disadvantage to their own nations. There is, as is invariably so with economics, no agreement on just how damaging to economies a policy to drastically reduce dependence upon fossil fuels would be.

One recently expressed view is that any economic downturn would not be long lasting, and that the fears of the consequences of full compliance with the Kyoto resolutions are much exaggerated. According to a report in *New Scientist* (15 June 2002, p.6) an economic analysis by S Schneider and C Azar largely contradicts the common assumption that a planned and determined international effort to progressively replace hydrocarbon fuels with other less polluting means of supplying energy for human needs would severely cripple economic growth and wealth accumulation in the USA. At worst there need be only a period of economic stagnation, which would soon be followed by a resurgence of economic growth. The growth then would be much less harmful to humanity generally, including the citizenship of the USA. Perhaps the sources of the salaries of economists also need to be taken into consideration in weighing the merits of conflicting opinions.

Taking all pros and cons into account, it would seem that the only responsible line of action to take is that of a wise but cautious medical practitioner: treat for the worst diagnosis while hoping for a better one. Rather than waiting until the debates are settled on whether a human activity is responsible for global warming, and whether the abandonment of fossil fuel dependence would have dire economic consequences, every effort should now be made to seek alternative energy supplies and to constrain the dimensions of the human population.

Whether or not the combustion of large quantities of hydrocarbons materials is the cause of the rise in mean surface temperature, the eventual abandonment of fossil fuels, and their replacement with the employment of other energy sources, would be no bad thing.

While there may be hydrocarbon deposits beneath the oceans (and they may be difficult to gain access to), known oil and gas fields may become exhausted within the next half-century. Thus, in any case, we should now be concentrating our minds on the harnessing of alternative energy sources. These are discussed in the next chapter.

Even if that transition can be effected without further prevarication and delay, it is unlikely that the currently occurring temperature rise could be halted in time to spare hardship to many human beings, as habitable land and food supplies shrink. In pressing for urgent action in an attempt to control the rate of rise of global temperature, and its many consequences, it is essential to emphasise that this alone will not be sufficient to ease our pending ills. Unless the imbalance between human populations and their food supplies is addressed with equal determination, all our oft-stated Benthamite aspirations to a world in which maximum happiness can be granted to the maximum number of persons, will come to naught.

The Risk of an Environment Destabilisation with Rapid and Serious Consequences

It is now increasingly difficult to deny that climatic changes are occurring; that these relate to global warming, and that global warming is largely, if not entirely, a consequence of human activities. There is still, it seems, the confident expectation of many that even if all this is so, the effects will become manifest only gradually. Thus there will be time enough in which to make any necessary adjustments to our lifestyles. The possibility of a quite sudden and catastrophic destabilisation of worldwide or regional ecosystems has been voiced from time to time, but has been regarded as an extravagant, even fanciful, exercise of the imagination, that need not be taken too seriously.

Anything as complex as the global environment is bound to have counteractions which moderate the effects of environmental disturbances. A proffered example of this is the uptake of atmospheric carbon dioxide by the oceans, by which not all the CO_2 released into the atmosphere stays there for all time hence. The pending danger of relying on a buffering action to mitigate the consequences of ongoing disturbances is that buffers are of finite capacity, and there may be little indication of the approach to the exhaustion of the buffering capacity. This may cease abruptly, and a hitherto masked effect of the disturbance will then suddenly appear. The saturation of an environmental buffering action could trigger a sequence of imbalances, and a whole ecosystem could then become destabilised. This is possible because the components of an environment are not independent contributors to it, but are contributors to an integrated complexity in dynamic equilibrium.

There is alarming evidence that just such a scenario could be well on the way to actually occurring. There are indications that, as a consequence of global warming, the Gulf Stream could cease to flow. The Gulf Stream brings warm water across the Atlantic Ocean from the Gulf of Mexico in a north-easterly direction, and it is this that makes, and keeps, northern European climates more temperate than they would otherwise be at that latitude. The Stream, the geophysicists tell us, is a continuous cyclic phenomenon. When the warm but cooling stream reaches an area between north Europe and Greenland, an effect of its cooling is that it sinks into deeper waters, at which level it flows back to the Gulf region where it picks up heat again, thus sustaining the warm water migration across the Atlantic.

There is now ample evidence that the northern Greenland ice cap is melting, as is occurring to ice formations in other parts of the world where ice has accumulated. The melted ice reaches the sea, and thereby contributes to a rising sea level. It does something else, too. It lowers the salinity of the sea water close to where the melted ice enters the sea, more so than elsewhere when mixing has occurred. This effect is magnified by the outflow from north-flowing Siberian rivers into the same Oceanic region.

Models of climatic change indicate that the flow in these rivers will increase because of the expected increased rainfall over Siberia as global warming proceeds. Those who know these things believe that the regionally reduced salinity will prevent the sinking of the Gulf Stream water masses. If this occurs, it will cut off the return flow to the Gulf which, in turn, will stop the flow of the warm Gulf Stream towards northern Europe. The anticipated effect of this would be that the winters of Northern Europe could become as cold as those of Alaska.

The consequences would not be just much colder winters and changes in the coastline as the sea level rises. Coastal land used for agriculture and habitation would be surrendered to the sea and agricultural yields generally could be reduced. Thus Britain, for example, would most likely be unable to sustain its present population density. If there is nowhere to which to migrate, a population crash may then be inevitable. If mass migration southwards is attempted, this would be unlikely to be politically trouble-free.

It is too early to say, with any certainty, whether this prognosis will be sustained or faulted by further studies. It should not, however, be dismissed simply because it is presently unproven. Whatever the verdict, this proposition is a salutary reminder of the complexity and the fragility of the environment that we are now abusing on quite massive scales. We could be heading for other unpleasant surprises, for climate models remain essentially simplistic, for all their complexity. They may now be quite accurate predictions of the environmental changes that can be expected, but only provided there is no unforeseen, and maybe as yet unforeseeable, sequences of secondary effects that could upset the calculations. The particular hazard is that the saturation of a buffer system triggers a whole sequences of secondary effects. It is, then, thoroughly irresponsible to argue, as the captains of capitalist industry are wont to do, that there is no point in moderating our injurious impacts upon ecosystems until there is absolutely no doubt about both the cause of global warming and the full spectrum of its effects. That ruthless expression of immediate self-interest is too dangerous to be left unchallenged.

Chapter Eight
ALTERNATIVE ENERGY SOURCES

First Considerations

It should now be clear that the eventual abandonment of resurfaced hydrocarbons as the principal source of energy is becoming increasingly imperative. What needs to be done to achieve that end is substantially more than was contained in the 1997 Kyoto inter-government agreement to stem carbon dioxide emission worldwide. Even if that agreement had been promptly ratified and implemented by the governments of all the most heavily industrialised and mechanised countries, it is most unlikely that the resultant reduction in carbon dioxide emissions would have been adequate to halt the global warming. This is not only because the proposal was far too conservative. It is also because while populations are still increasing in many regions of the world, many states still low down in the economic hierarchy are seeking to raise their living standards by developing marketable industries. Indeed it is reported in the *New Scientist* (14 April 2004, p.17) that although

> China has signed up to the Kyoto protocol, its rapidly growing economy is heavily reliant on coal, which is the worst fuel in terms of CO_2 emissions. It plans to almost treble the capacity of its coal-fired stations by 2020.

Thus the likelihood is that even had the Kyoto proposals been fully and promptly implemented, atmospheric carbon dioxide emission would have continued to rise, and global warming and all its consequences would have proceeded on its potentially disastrous course. At best the prompt implementation of the

Kyoto proposals would have bought only a little time in which to order our relations with the changing ecosystem of which we are part, and upon which we depend.

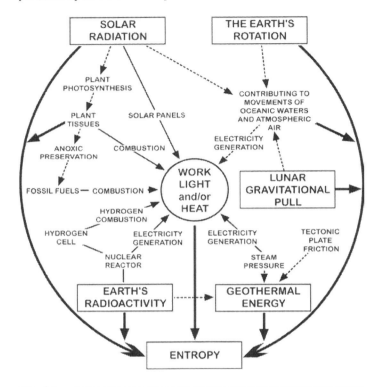

FIG. 8.1 A DIAGRAMMATIC SUMMARY OF THE ENERGY SOURCES AND FLOWS THAT CAN BE HARNESSED AND USED TO PROVIDE HEAT AND LIGHT, AND TO DO USEFUL WORK. THICK LINES INDICATE NATURAL ENERGY FLOWS FROM SOURCE TO ENTROPY; BROKEN LINES INDICATE NATURAL ENERGY TRANSFERS; AND THIN LINES INDICATE DIVERSIONS OF ENERGY FLOW BY HUMAN ENDEAVOURS TO DO WORK OR FOR LIGHT AND/OR HEAT PRODUCTION.

Alternative Sources of Energy

Fig. 8.1 seeks to express the prime sources of energy which are continuously flowing from a high potential towards that lowest possible energy potential called entropy (see footnote p.125). These energy flows are occurring all the time whether or not they are tapped and directed to the execution of work, or to the creation of light and heat. They are the sun; the radioactivity of Earth's crust; the rotation of the planet, and the gravitation pull of the Earth's satellite, the Moon. The outer curved pathways in Fig. 8.1 represent the continuous natural flows of energy to entropy when they are not intercepted and put to use. The centripetal pathways indicate the human interventions by which these energy flows can be put to human use.

The alternative energy flows that could be, and in some cases are being, directed to satisfy human energy needs for industry, home and transport are considered in turn below. They are generally referred to collectively as 'renewable energy' although that term is hardly appropriate since naturally there is no such thing as reusable or renewable energy. Energy can only be used once as it flows down its energy gradient towards entropy. Once energy is at too low a potential to be useable it would have to be pumped back up to a higher potential to be used again to do useful work. That, however, would require a greater energy input than would then be available for reuse. The term *renewable energy*, as used in this context, seeks to distinguish between the essentially irreplaceable molecular energy of the hydrocarbon deposits, and those naturally and ceaselessly occurring releases of energy which then flow down energy gradients until they can flow no further, whether or not the flow is intercepted and put to use. These flows will not continue forever, because the Earth itself is not forever, but certainly for so long as there is life on Earth. In that sense they are inexhaustible. In theory at least, and perhaps to some extent in practice too, all these continuously ongoing energy flows can be harnessed and put to work at they flow to entropy. The methods of harnessing these energy flows could be environmentally harmful, just as coal mining, peat cutting, oil drilling and woodcutting can be, but the use of these energy sources does not itself cause environmental damage, because the energy flow to entropy will occur whether or not it is harnessed and put to work.

i) Solar Energy

What is achieved by plants when they trap solar energy and convert it into the molecular energy of their own substance is also achievable by relatively simple engineered physical means. When solar energy radiation falls upon solar panels some of the incoming energy is absorbed by the panel material. The energy may then be converted into heat which can be piped away for storage in a well-insulated mass such as a tank of water, for later use as a heat supply. Alternatively when solar radiant energy falls on to a photovoltaic panel it becomes converted into a flow of electricity. This can be put to immediate use as light or heat, or to do work, or it can be further converted into molecular (or chemical) energy in a battery of cells for later use. It is also now being mooted that solar panels could be linked to fuel cells in which the solar energy is employed in the generation of hydrogen. Hydrogen, the combustion of which yields only water, can then be used as a transportable and pollution-free fuel. (See the section below on hydrogen as a fuel.)

Because solar panels, like leaves, must be exposed to sunlight, they could compete with plants for places in the sun. Since food production is a primary necessity it must take priority over the placement of physical solar panels where the land is fertile and can be put to agricultural use. There are however vast areas, such as arid deserts, which are quite unsuitable for the growth of vegetation, and there is an abundance of rooftops on which solar panels could be installed to contribute to, or even fully meet, the energy needs of the premises; or the power could be fed, as an electric current flow, into a grid system for a wider distribution. Solar panel technology is improving all the time, and the solar panel market is expanding rapidly. In consequence, the installation cost is falling, and electricity generation by solar energy entrapment is becoming attractive not only because its direct use does not pollute the environment, but also because of it becoming economically competitive with other power supplies.

With the further development of the physical entrapment of

solar energy, there could be a considerable reduction in the need for electricity to be generated from fossil fuels. Solar energy entrapment alone, however, is unlikely to become a total substitute for the burning of fossil fuels. This is because, like the use of wind power to produce electricity (see below), production will vary from day to night, and from day to day. Added to a more stable supply of electricity, however, it is a potentially valuable contributor to much needed alternatives to the use of mined hydrocarbons.

ii) The Radioactivity of Planet Earth

Another energy flow which, like that of solar radiation, is occurring spontaneously and continuously, is that of waves and particles emitted from radioactive materials in the Earth's crust, as the radioactivity decays. Like any other energy flow, it can be intercepted and converted into energy for human usage. Unlike the molecular energy of hydrocarbon deposits, the nuclear energy of the radioactive elements within the Earth's crust was not created by the earlier entrapment of solar radiation. The radioactive material has been present right from the stellar origin of the Earth, and its decay in the confines of the Earth's interior is believed to be a substantial contributor to the high temperatures beneath the Earth's crust. Also, like other spontaneous energy flows, and unlike the energy of stable molecular structures, the energy of natural radioactivity cannot be conserved if it is not being harnessed to do useful work, although in a nuclear power station the rate of energy release is accelerated. The wave and particle energy is being continuously emitted at whatever level and rate is a property of the particular radioactive element, and its natural concentration within the substance of the Earth. The substance in which uranium is present in readily extractable quantities is pitchblende. As with most other usable elements and materials, it is more concentrated in some places than in others, the sites suitable for exploitation being identified by geologists.

Workable pitchblende deposits are known and mined in parts of Russia, USA, Canada, Australia and South Africa. Radioactivity, however, is not confined to the places where pitchblende occurs in exploitable quantities. In some locations, particularly where there are granite rock formations close to the

Earth's surface, the radioactive gas, radon, seeps out into the atmosphere. As a contribution to the natural radioactivity to which all life forms are exposed, this is generally not particularly harmful. When, however, buildings are erected on such land, radon can accumulate within the buildings if they are inadequately ventilated, and this can harm to the inhabitants. Because of the widespread occurrence of low levels of radiation. It has been said that possibly as much subterranean radioactive material has been brought to the surface by coal mining as by pitchblende mining, but it remains unconcentrated. Even so, radiation from open coal fires may have augmented the level of human exposure to radiation. A point that needs to be stressed, when considering the harmful effects of exposure to radiation, is that all living creatures evolved on this radioactive planet, and are exposed to a background level of radiation throughout their lives.

Nowhere accessible is the naturally occurring radioactive material sufficiently concentrated for its emission to be captured and used to do work. For any such purpose the radioactive elements must be extracted from the material of the Earth's crust in which it occurs and brought together into a usable mass. Most (more than 99%) of the uranium extractable from pitchblende is the non-radioactive isotope with an atomic weight of 238 (U^{238}). Only about 0.7% of the uranium in pitchblende is the unstable isotope U^{235}. Thus when the uranium is extracted from the pitchblende as a mixture of U^{238} and U^{235} it is not highly radioactive, and the intensity of its spontaneously emission of charged particles is low. When U^{235} is bombarded with neutrons, however, it will split (fission) with the expulsion of 2-3 neutrons. Thus if the U^{235} in the uranium is separated out and the amount of U^{235} in the uranium raised to about 5%, a chain reaction can be started, with expulsion of neutrons causing ever more U^{235} atoms to expel neutrons. The passage of the expelled neutrons is slowed down so that they do not bounce off other U^{235} atoms, but penetrate them, producing the neutron emissions from them. These neutrons will then act on other U^{235} atoms.

The chain reaction needs to be caused to occur at a controlled rate, and the reaction is moderated by interspersed graphite rods which absorb neutrons. With each fission, energy is released and appears as heat, which is maintained at the level required for the operation of a nuclear reactor by the automatic raising and lowering of the graphite rods. The heat is conducted away from the reactor by a continuous closed fluid (liquid or gas) circulation. The heat is then transferred, via a heat exchanger, into a secondary closed circulation of water, and it is the heat-induced pressure in this secondary circulation which is used to drive the turbines of the electricity generators. The fission can be sustained for so long as the concentration of U^{235} in the rods remains high enough. In prescribed circumstances the fission process will remain sufficient for the electricity generation process to continue at a steady rate for some two years before the fuel rods become depleted of U^{235} and need to be replaced.

One tonne of this atomic fuel will produce the same amount of electricity as could result from the combustion of some 70,000 tonnes of coal, and does so without polluting the atmosphere with carbon dioxide. If more heat is generated than the primary circulation can remove, either because the graphite rods are incorrectly positioned, or the heat is not being continuously removed because of a misfunction to the heat removal circulation, the uranium fuel rods could melt, and/or the heat-induced increased pressure within the circulatory system could cause the pipes to rupture. Radioactive material could then be discharged into the atmosphere and become dispersed over a wide area. This, in essence, is what occurred at Chernobyl, when the meltdown of the fuel and the explosion of the overheated coolant occurred. It occurred because of an inexcusable and avoidable human error, although the particular design of the nuclear power plant may have played a part in what occurred.

In principle, then, converting the energy released by the accelerated rate of fission of U^{235} into electricity is, like the use of solar radiation, waves, tide or air movement, the utilisation of an energy flow which occurs naturally, although at a slower rate. As with other utilisations of naturally occurring energy flows, there need be no atmospheric pollution-provided there is no mishap in the operation of the reactors.

The possibility of mishaps involving the accidental release of radioactive material into the atmosphere is one of two major reasons for the popular misgivings about the wisdom of continuing to construct and operate nuclear-fuelled electricity generators. The other reason is that the safe disposal of radioactive waste is seemingly problematic. This second objection is discussed below. First, the risk of further nuclear power plant mishaps must be considered. Although there have been three major serious nuclear mishaps, the most serious and consequential of which was that at Chernobyl in Belarus, it must be emphasised that all of these accidents were attributable to readily preventable human operational errors, which should never have occurred. Nuclear-fuelled power generators, properly and competently managed, are now very safe indeed. All manner of duplicated control systems virtually eliminate the possibility of failures to position the graphite rods correctly, and of a failure of the process of heat removal. Many other installations have been operating accident-free for many years, and are contributing substantially both to power needs and to the reduction in environmental pollution. Indeed, the safety records at these installations are better than those of many other industrial processes, and are greatly better than those of mining for fossil fuels and drilling for oil. In France, for example, some 70% of its electricity requirements have been provided by nuclear installation for many years without mishap, and without the fears and protests of the citizenship.

An abiding problem is the safe disposal of the waste products of nuclear power generation, some of which will remain highly radioactive for hundred of years. The basis of the problem is that much of the residual radioactivity is not just from the 2 to 3% of U^{235} still contained in the spent rods. This can be recovered and used in the making of new fuel rods, or can be diluted by mixing with inert mining residues and safely returned underground, where it need be no more dangerous than the pitchblende from which it was first obtained. There are, however, other highly radioactive materials in the spent fuel rods, which complicate either of the above two procedures. The spent rods contain some 1% of highly radioactive plutonium (Pu^{239}) and lesser amounts of highly radioactive strontium (Sr^{90}) and caesium (Cs^{137}). The complete separation of these from the less radioactive residue is difficult to achieve. In a recovery and/or disposal installation such as that at Sellafield in the UK, much of the U^{235} and Pu^{239} could be isolated separately and reprocessed for further use as nuclear fuel. The Pu^{239}, when converted into the safer Pu^{239} oxide, can be incorporated into rods of a mixed oxide fuel (MOX), which could be used in a new generation of nuclear installations known as Fast Breeder Reactors.

These recovery processes still leave quantities of substances of both low-level and high-level radioactivity to be disposed of safely. When suitably encased in durable cladding, the deep burial of the highly radioactive material would surely be safer than leaving the material lying about for centuries on, or close to, the Earth's surface. Widespread public concern for safety, encouraged by the more emotional than reasoned opposition of groups which are as wholly opposed to the use of nuclear energy for peaceful purposes as they are for military purposes, is frustrating every attempt to resolve this waste disposal problem. The solution preferred by the body responsible for the care of this material in the UK (NIREX) would be to place the suitably encased material in bunkers some 300 metres below the surface. By continuous monitoring, any leakage of radioactivity could be quickly detected, reached and remedied. At that depth the material would be well below subterranean aquifers, thus eliminating the risk of water contamination. Also, at that depth an earthquake would be unlikely to rupture the cladding and cause the release of radioactive material, since the worst movements during earthquakes occur much nearer to the surface. Furthermore, in any future ice age, the scouring of land by glacial movements would not extend deep enough to cause a leakage of radiation. The nuclear waste in the UK is still stored as safely as is possible in this circumstance of indecision, but close to the surface, with all the risks of radiation leakage that deep cavern storage would eliminate. What must be evident to all thinking and informed persons is that the risks that we are taking by procrastinating is far greater than any risks that deep storage would present.

Absolute safety is not something that can be enjoyed with absolute certainty, and in every circumstance. Life is beset with far more likely life-threatening hazards than that of exposure to radioactivity. Even if the hazards of travelling on foot, bicycle, automobile, plane, or train; of tobacco smoking and alcohol consumption, and of the side effects of both prescribed and unprescribed drugs, are avoided, accidents in the home are high on the list of other perils to which we are each exposed daily. Infectious diseases such as tuberculosis and malaria, and idiopathic conditions such as cancer, remain major causes of premature demise. Even if one is not visited by any of these misfortunes, earthquakes and harvest failures due to exceptional climatic conditions contribute to the ever-present uncertainty about one's personal safety. In comparison, the risk of a mishap in the storage of radioactive waste material when all reasonable precautions are taken, is too small to be the subject of so much mass hysteria. Furthermore, the risks involved in all aspects of nuclear energy usage are utterly insignificant when compare with suffering that mankind is bringing upon itself by its excessive procreation and the burning of fossil fuels.

In the UK public opinion is mostly inadequately informed, and this handicaps the resolution of the problem. Better progress is being made elsewhere. In France, where there is less public fear, the government has gone ahead with the safe deep storage of its radioactive waste material. In Sweden, where public opinion can never be ignored, the public, it seems, is well informed and has an intelligent awareness of its social responsibility.

With the continuing public concern, especially perhaps in the UK, it is arguable that the abandonment of the use of radioactive material as an energy source would be prudent if one's concern is solely with oneself, and one's own lifetime. That, however, would be to abandon any concern for the welfare of succeeding generations. There can now be little doubt that our descendants will curse us for our reluctance to abandon the use of hydrocarbon deposits as our principal energy source. The sooner we now do so, the better. Eventually it may be possible to satisfy all our energy needs by harnessing the energy flows of solar radiation and the movements of air and water, which are essentially pollution-free. In the meanwhile it would be far safer for mankind to be less fearful of nuclear power and less blinded by contemporary economics. Humanity would be better served now by extending the use of the Earth's radioactivity as a principal constant energy source, than by staying with hydrocarbon materials until either they have become exhausted, or the consequences have become intolerable and irreversible.

Even with the small risk now of an untoward leakage from stored radioactive waste, the overall operation of nuclear power generators is only a minor threat to life. In the United Kingdom there has been no death proven to be the result of a nuclear reactor explosion or of an accidental or unauthorised radiation leak. Since the hazards associated with nuclear waste disposal are well known, when adequate precautions are taken, there is no reason why nuclear waste disposal should give rise to a single death. In contrast, bronchitis caused by the atmospheric pollution when fossil fuels are burned has an annual death toll running into thousands.

To favour the extension, rather than the contraction, of nuclear-fuelled electricity generation, is not to advocate a headlong rush to proliferate whatever existing systems now seems to be safe, without continuing research and development to achieve even greater safety and efficiency. There need not be a permanent dependence on nuclear-fuelled power generation unless experience shows that this is the best way of providing a continuous background energy supply to underpin the other harnessable but variable natural energy flows.

To put the current level of additional exposure to radiation attributable to human exploitation of the Earth's radioactivity into perspective, it is noteworthy that some 85.5% of the radiation to which Earth dwellers are exposed comes from natural emissions such as radon gas and gamma particles from soils and rocks, and cosmic radiation. We voluntarily increase our exposure to radiation every time we fly at high altitudes, and subject ourselves to X-radiation for medical reasons. These exposures amount to another 14% or thereabouts of our total exposure. This adds up to about 99.5% of the exposure to radiation to which human beings are exposed. The sum of the exposure attributable to fallout from nuclear weapon tests, and industrial applications is about 0.4% of the total, while exposure to nuclear energy discharges currently amount to only 0.1% or one thousandths of our total exposure.

With adequate care, this last figure need never be substantially higher, and is clearly of little significance when compared with other inescapable exposures.

An as yet unmentioned but substantial objection to nuclear power generation is that on current bases of calculation it cannot compete economically with power obtained from the combustion of fossil fuels. If only installation and energy generation costs are charged to consumers, the difference between costs is not great. When, however, the costs of decommissioning retired nuclear power stations, and of disposing of nuclear wastes, are included in the calculation, it is true that nuclear-fuelled power generation is relatively expensive.

In the UK the eventual cost of decommissioning nuclear installations at the end of years of service, had been recognised by the now defunct UK Electricity Generating Authority, and financial provision for this outlay had been made in the industry's long-term budgeting. Funds were set aside for that purpose and were invested as earmarked capital within the industry's range of activities. When the electricity generating industry was broken up by the government of the day, and sold piecemeal, and cheaply so, to commercial operators, these earmarked investment funds were lost with no reservation of funds for decommissioning to enable the financially separated nuclear power division to do so as planned. The complaint was then made that the separated nuclear generating body would be unable to finance the decommissioning and at the same time keep the cost of nuclear powered electricity generation competitive with that of fossil fuel-derived electrical energy. Now that the government has to subsidise the decommissioning operations substantially, it can be seen how irresponsible was the piecemeal sell-off of the electricity generating industry to private enterprise.

Even if this economic nobbling of Britain's nuclear power industry must now be treated as a *fait accompli*, there is still an unaddressed unfairness in the calculation of relative production costs. The fossil fuel industry is the major cause of the environmental damage now leading to global warming. If that industry was to be required to repair the environmental damage that it causes, or to pay compensation for the damage that it cannot repair, the differential in production costs would disappear or, more likely, swing the other way. Most likely nuclear power generation would then be seen to be not only less environmentally damaging than is the use of fossil fuels, but also more economic.

There must be the suspicion that the difficulty of disposing of radioactive waste products has been exaggerated by those with competitive commercial interests. It is possible, and even likely, that the well-intentioned, though often emotionally blinded and ill-informed 'Greens' have become, to some extent at least, the unwitting allies of the fossil fuel industries. By their opposition to the use of radioactivity which, like wind and water flows, is occurring whether or not it is put to use, those who are opposed to nuclear-fuelled electricity generation on environmental grounds are helping to sustain the fossil fuel industries, and the environmental damage that it is doing.

It is unlikely that the safe production, usage and disposal of nuclear fuel residues is beyond the wit of man, and James Lovelock (proponent of the Gaia theory) has expressed the view that we should never have stopped building nuclear power stations. He would, he has said, gladly allow some of the lower grade radioactive waste to be buried (suitably encapsulated) in his garden. This, he avers, would be virtually harmless, and could be used to supply the energy needs of his household, cheaply and in an environmentally pollution-less way. Certainly the risk to his health would be far less than that of living in a house built on radon-emitting granite. In making this statement Lovelock would seem to have anticipated the development of a small safe reactor that could be housed in the basement of any building, to provide all the energy needs of the building (see *New Scientist*, 25 August 2001). The fuel is ceramic-coated uranium oxide pebbles which only need to be replaced at intervals of about ten years. The mass of radioactive material is far too small for a runaway meltdown to be possible. The only risk would be a radiation leak, which could be readily and rapidly detected by a monitor, and contained. With adequate development before marketing this small nuclear-powered electricity generator, the occupants of the premises would be at less risk than that resulting from an inadequately serviced gas appliances, while the benefit to planetary residents generally could be vast.

Clearly there is a strong case for an objective reappraisal of the pros and cons of a resurgence of nuclear-fuelled electricity generation. The remote possibility of further accidents remains, but that risk is now much diminished since the lessons from those accidents that have occurred have been well learned. On the other hand, the continued dependence upon fossil fuels is bound, sooner or later, to be disastrous. It will be the cause of human suffering on a far vaster scale than even a major nuclear reactor accident could give rise to.

The postscript must now be added that nuclear power stations could be terrorist targets. That is true, and is worrisome, but the water supplies to big cities are equally or more vulnerable to attack, and the consequences could be every bit as disastrous. The danger of too many people all trying to live equally well on finite resources is every bit as dangerous, and far more certain to be ultimately disastrous.

My conclusion, then, is that it is the oil magnates, not the Friends of the Earth, and the parents of the next few human generations who have good reason to be pleased with the shrinking of the nuclear power industry. Global warming is occurring, and it is all but certain that most, if not all of this is the consequence of the burning of combustible fossil substances on a massive scale, and other human exploitations of the substances of the Earth. Just the predicted rise in sea level should be enough to alert us to the dangers ahead if we do not mend our ways. It is reported by Abramovitz (2001), that in Bangladesh alone, the rise in sea level of 0.5 metres, which is now certain to occur in the course of the twenty-first century, will result in the loss of nearly 30,000 square kilometres of farmed and inhabited land, and the displacement of 50 million persons. In Europe, the Netherlands alone will lose about 2,200 square kilometres of land, and 10 million persons will be displaced. The resultant hunger and conflicts that will surely occur as land for food and habitation is lost, will result in many more deaths than is ever likely to result from the continued development of nuclear-fuelled production of usable energy. By failing to weigh the risks of a dependency on nuclear-fuelled energy and on hydrocarbon-fuelled energy we have, I believe, missed a great opportunity to spare both the environment and the welfare of future generations, while techniques for harnessing the energy of movements of oceanic water and atmospheric air are being developed. If we had persevered with the development of proven techniques for the safe conversion of nuclear energy into usable power we could by now have substantially reduced fossil fuel usage, carbon dioxide emissions and extent of the global warming. There may still be time to slow our progression towards ultimate disaster, and to achieve that the harnessing of the Earth's natural radiation remains an option worthy of urgent reconsideration.

This disproportionately detailed discussion of nuclear power is to temper the popular opposition to it, some of which may be reasoned and objective, but much of which is not.

iii) Wind, Wave and Tidal Movements

As is indicated in Fig. 8.1, energy of other origins becomes translated into the kinetic energies of atmospheric movement (wind) and oceanic movement (tides and waves). These are the energy flows resulting from the inter-acting influences of Earth's rotation and solar radiation, and changes in the gravitational effect of the moon as the Earth rotates. The primary energy translations into the motions of the atmosphere and the oceans are far more complex than this account indicates, but these complexities are immaterial to the present consideration. Here the concern is with the natural and constantly occurring energy flows and fluxes of the atmosphere and oceans that are potentially capable of being harnessed and converted into energy forms that can be used for doing work, and providing heat and light. Once adequately developed, these energy conversion processes could eliminate the present dependence on the fossil fuels.

It has long been the ambition of engineers to arrest the kinetic energies of the wave movements and tidal flows, and the obvious way of doing so is to use the directional water flows, to turn the turbines of electricity generators, or to cause them to operate mechanical devices, such as milling machines. Many attempts have been made to use these naturally occurring energy flows for the generation of electricity in this way, but these have been frustrated by technical difficulties. These relate largely to the capricious temperaments of the seas ranging from tranquillity to tempest, with little prior warning of change.

The successful harnessing of waves and tides will need robust structures and much research. Venture capital tends to flow towards projects most likely to yield quicker returns, and consequently the financing of research and development on means of converting tides and waves into useable energy has largely ceased. The conversion of even a very small proportion of these kinetic energy flows into useful work or into electricity, however, could contribute, in a lasting and environmentally harmless way, to the eventual abandonment of the use of fossil fuels. Thus despite the disappointing return on money spent on research and development hitherto, the continuation of adequately financed research would be a wise investment. A strong case could be made for greater contributions from public purses.

iv) The Return of Precipitated Water to the Oceans

The employment of the force of rain-derived fresh water as it runs off high lands and back towards the sea is the most fully developed of the processes of diverting the kinetic energy of natural flows into energy forms suitable for human usage. Before the development of steam power, and then electrical energy, the flow of rivers and streams was used to drive machinery for grinding grain, and for other industrial operations. With the development of electricity generation by rotating armatures, the use of the pressure of moving fluid to turn the turbine blades of dynamos became an energy source for industry. Steam pressure in an enclosed system created by the energy released by burning organic matter, or in a nuclear reactor, is one way of achieving this. The flow of water from the high potential of mountains and hills to the low potential of the sea is another. This conversion of the kinetic energy of water flow into electricity is greatly enhanced when a good head of water is created by causing water to accumulate behind a dam. This increased head of water on the upside side of the dam not only creates the pressure needed to drive the turbines of the electricity generators, but evens out the otherwise seasonal strength of water flow. Now, almost everywhere that a dam could be built, and operated efficiently and economically, one has been built. Hydroelectricity, as this is called, contributes greatly to human energy needs without polluting the atmosphere; and can be readily distributed by overhead cables to improve the quality of life and industrial development of, often, hitherto undeveloped territories.

There is reason to be concerned about the long-term safety of some dams, and also about the ecological, political and sociological ramifications and consequences of some of them. Where a river flows through more than one country, a dam may serve the up-stream country well, but seriously damage the ecology and life-support economy and habitability of the downstream country. There is also concern about the duration of the usefulness of some of hydroelectric installations. In some parts of the world, such as the relatively unpopulated lands in northern territories of the Quebec Province of Canada, the ecological disturbances caused by hydroelectric installations are minor in comparison with the environmental damage caused by fossil fuel consumption. Elsewhere, as with the blockade of the Nile by the Aswan Dam in Egypt, the rapid accumulation of silt behind the dam may not only diminish the effective life of the scheme; but evaporation from surface of the large expanse of water behind the dam has been reported to be almost equal to the inflow from the White and Blue Nile rivers. The reduced flow below the dam has affected both agriculture and public health between Aswan and the Nile delta.

Clearly hydroelectric schemes are not problem-free. With due consideration of the other social and political consequences of dam construction, this harnessing of an energy flow which would otherwise be unused, is a valuable contribution to the replacement or avoidance of fossil fuel consumption. While the benefit of hydroelectricity generation is environmentally preferable to hydrocarbon-fuelled electricity generation, there is little scope for its extension, as suitable and accessible, but still undeveloped sites are now quite limited. There are, however, still plenty of opportunities for the construction of small 'low head' dams. These may not be able to contributions substantially to a grid system of power distribution over a wide area, but could serve local needs well. Wherever there are now disused millponds and wherever new millponds could be constructed, the water flow could be put to use to create a local electricity supply. The ecological consequences of a proliferation of 'low head' dams, however, would need to be considered in the first place.

v) Wind Power

The kinetic energy of atmospheric air movement was widely employed to operate milling machinery and water pumps before the advent of coal-fired steam power. The distribution of electricity generated from the energy released from fossil fuels, led to the demise of most windmills and wind-pumps. One of the reasons for this demise of a local and free energy source was the variability of the wind force and, therefore, of the amount of energy that could be harvested and put to immediate use. Small wind turbines are, however, still used widely in remote areas not served by an electricity distribution grid, both for general domestic and farmstead needs, and to pump subterranean aquifer water to the surface. Only relatively recently has there been the development of large wind-driven turbines that can generate electricity in a sufficient quantity for it to be fed into a distribution grid. Often several such turbines are placed together on exposed land, or above shallow waters. Design research continues and public objections to the sight of them, and the noise they make, seem to be on the wane, as public awareness of the need for them increases. The problem of the variability of the wind strength, and therefore of the amount of electricity that can be generated, means that this mode of electricity generation needs to be linked to another continuously sustainable process of electricity generation. This can be, and generally is, provided by fossil-fuel-burning generators, particularly the newer ones that burn hydrocarbon gas. The contentment with this partnership implies a hope that hydrocarbon gas is an inexhaustible fuel supply. This cannot be so, and for this reason, additional to that of the environmental pollution caused by burning gas, an alternative continuously sustainable means of electricity generator should be sought and implemented. But for the popular fear of it, which is not entirely without foundation, but which is unlikely to be any greater than the many other hazards we must live with, nuclear-fuelled electricity generation is tailor-made for that role. As with the burning of fossil fuels, a problematic residue is left, but not one that is so damaging and its disposal so irresolute as that of spewing six billion tons or more of CO_2 in the atmosphere every year.

vi) Sub-surface Heat

Another harnessable and employable energy flow is that which results from the geothermal effects of deeply sub-surface radioactivity and the frictional heat of tectonic plate collisions. Which of these processes is the principal contributor to the harnessable geothermal heat is not material here. What matters is that there is harnessable heat close to the Earth's surface in some locations such as Iceland, New Zealand and Hawaii. As with the other energy sources and flows discussed above, both the production and the dissipation of this thermal energy will occur whether or not it is harnessed and usefully employed. Because of the remoteness of the places where near-surface geothermal heat is most abundant, there has hitherto been little interest in the commercial exploitation of geothermal heat as a usable energy source. This could change, since there is now an interest in the use of hydrogen as a 'clean' and transportable fuel. The promise of a pollution-free fuel, because the burning of hydrogen produces only water, sounds too good to be true, and indeed, it is.

Hydrogen, unlike the natural energy resources discussed in this chapter, is not there for the taking. It has to be produced, usually by splitting water molecules into hydrogen and oxygen (hydrolysis). This needs an energy input, and the efficiency of the production process is bound to considerably less that 100%. Thus if the hydrogen is produced by burning a fossil fuel, the use of hydrogen as a fuel will still involve a considerable degree of atmospheric pollution. The suggestion has been made that geothermal heat could be used in the production of hydrogen, which could then be transported, much as petroleum products are now, to where it is required. That development would be of great economic benefit to places where geothermal heat is readily extractable, but before that could become a large-scale commercial undertaking the problems of the transporting, storing and distributing hydrogen safely have to be resolved.

Concluding Comment

This brief survey of energy sources and their uses admittedly lacks the authority that engineers and others directly engaged in the development of the use of what are called 'renewable energies' could bring to the subject. The purpose of this discussion is simply to outline the possible ways by which we could now be reducing our dependency on fossil fuels, by harnessing and using continuous natural energy flows. The major handicaps are lack of resolve and lack of capital for research, development and implementation. This is because both finance investors and voters look for quick returns that are of immediate benefit; and that is because the natural tendency to have a greater interest in the present than in the future. If there is to be a future worth contemplating, we will need to moderate our natural tendencies with constructive and responsible thought.

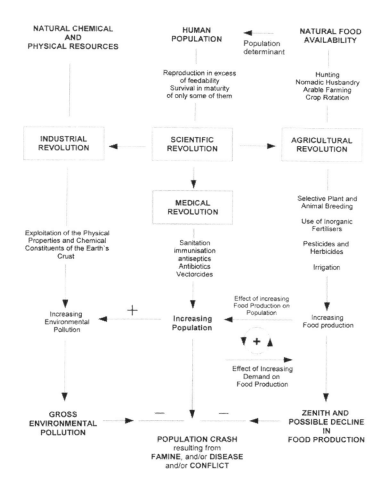

FIG. 9.1   A SUMMARY OF THE IMPACTS OF THE PURE AND APPLIED
SCIENTIFIC REVOLUTIONS UPON POPULATIONS, THEIR HEALTH
AND LONGEVITY, AND THEIR FOOD SUPPLIES.

161

Chapter Nine
THE FATAL INHERITANCE

The Three Basic Fatal Inheritances

Virtually all that has been considered in the preceding pages is outlined and integrated in Fig. 9.1, either overtly or covertly.

There are now many matters concerning the deteriorating state of the environment that greatly concerns some of us, and should concern all of us, for we are all affected by them. This deterioration has many facets which range from the extinction, and threatened extinction, of many other plant and animal species, the destruction of forest areas for timber extraction and for agricultural land usage; the depletions of oceanic fish stocks; the exhaustion and pollution of the water supplies of many communities, to the pollution of the atmosphere and the many now evident and threatening consequences of that. All this, and more, is not just the consequence of human activities, but of the activities of ever more humans engaged in a continuously expanding range of environmentally disturbing activities.

It might seem that we have only ourselves to blame for both our expanding numbers, and for the magnitude of these environmental disturbances. Some of these environmental exploitations are compelled by the need to provide food enough to sustain us all. Others are to satisfy the other needs, some of which are basic and others quite superficial, but are now widely perceived as imperative in order to sustain ever more extravagant and artificial lifestyles. 'Blame' however, is the wrong word, for that implies wilful intent. *All that has occurred is the consequence of what we are*. We are ruled by our instinctive patterns of behaviour, and by the capabilities of an evolved central nervous system, which facilitates the better execution of those instincts. It is the natural basic concern for self and the evolved ability to find ways to do anything and everything to the physical and biological materials of the Earth's crust that suits ourselves, that has got us to where we are today. But that is putting the cart before the horse.

Whatever circumstance accounts for the origin of life on Earth, it was the advent of the process of photosynthesis that made all the difference to life's progression. Only when living things had evolved the means of capturing the energy radiating from the sun could living systems proliferate and diversify, largely unconstrained by the limitation of earth-bound energy supplies. Thus the spread of vegetation, and then the evolution and spread of mobile harvesters which use the vegetation as their source of energy and bodybuilding materials. From these herbivorous organisms there then evolved carnivorous scavengers and predators that gained their energy third-hand or fourth-hand by eating animal tissues as their source of energy and bodybuilding materials. Food chains were thus created between the input of the energy of solar radiation and the ultimate flow of dissipated energy to entropy. The evolution of the mammals, and from them, the primates, was still a long way off.

The primate Homo sapiens may have evolved from a forest-dwelling fruit- and root-eating primate, which migrated onto open plains in search of food. There the edible vegetation was seasonal, but animal tissue was always available to predatory carnivores with the ability to capture and kill. With the clawed, fanged and agile carnivores already established in open territory, the ability of a primate to compete with them successfully most likely depended upon the evolution of the mental ability required to develop hunting techniques and strategies, and the manual skills required to make and use weapons of capture.

The densities of prehuman and human populations as harvesters and hunters were determined at all times by the extent of the food supply, and how much of that they could gain access to. That share of the natural food supply obtainable by Homo sapiens would have increased as the ability of Homo sapiens to outwit other competing species increased. There would then have been a slow progressive growth in human population sizes. Other circumstances, such as periods of drought or the epidemic spread of diseases, would have sometimes reduced populations to below the supportable levels, but in no circumstance, and at no time, could populations have been substantially above the numbers that the food supply could be support.

The proposition to which the title of this book, *The Fatal Inheritance,* refers is that there are three basic behavioural characteristics of animals generally: reproduction in excess of the possibility of the survival of all progeny into maturity; a prime interest in the survival of self but often also of one's still-dependent progeny; and belligerency in defence of that self-interest. These genetically fixed behavioural features are not only crucial for the survival of the individual organism in an intensely competitive environment, but are also essential to the process of evolution, by which organismic adaptation to the ever changing prevailing circumstances is effected. Evolution would not have continued as far as Homo sapiens without the retention of these behavioural phenotypic expressions of the genotype. They have not only persisted through aeons of evolution, but have been instrumental in effecting changes in the life forms as environments have changed. These behavioural inheritances, then, are not fatal to the continuation of life in one form or another, but, on the contrary, are essential to it. There is, however, never the guarantee that any one species can survive unchanged despite environmental changes. In the long-term life forms must be able to adapt to changing circumstances or die. The individuals of a species that survive in changed environmental circumstances are those genotypically, and therefore phenotypically, in harmony with the change, while other individuals less well suited become eliminated.

Since inheritable adaptations always involve the mass extermination of the unfit majority, the process of selection is never a cosy one to contemplate. This natural selection is unrecognisable as such at the time that it is operating. Every living thing eventually dies, and it is just that some live less long than others. Thus the evolutionary process can be recognised as such only retrospectively. Despite the endeavours of each individual of a species to defend itself, its food source and its progeny in a natural environment, many – perhaps the majority – of each generation do not survive for long enough to reproduce.

Premature extinction may be because they fail to find enough food and water, lack sufficient immunity to infection, or fail to escape predation. Whatever its cause, premature extinction means that the particular genomes of the non-survivors to maturity do not contribute to the genetic composition of successive generations. Only those individuals that are able to survive to maturity have any chance of doing that, and thereby to remain genome candidates in the eliminative process of natural selections by which evolutionary change is brought about.

These basic behavioural characteristics, which have persisted throughout the evolution of animals, cannot be lost in natural environments because they are major contributors to the process of natural selection upon which evolution and ultimate survival depends. They can, however, be weakened by deliberate selection, as has occurred in the selective breeding of pacific domesticated animals. Such unnatural selection leaves the pacified animals unsuited for survival in highly competitive, and often changing, natural environments, because they then lack the competitive edge essential to survival. These artificially selected animals, therefore, can have no long-term futures outside the protected synthetic environment for which they were bred. Likewise there is no natural process of selection by which Homo sapiens could have become likewise pacified. On the contrary, belligerency between tribes over land and food supplies has, it seems, become intensified in the human species, while the instincts to procreate excessively, and to be primarily concerned with self and self-preservation, have surely remained undiminished. As Erasmus Darwin, grandfather of Charles Darwin had noted, 'One great slaughterhouse, the warring world.' Charles Darwin paved the way to the understanding of why.

A Fourth Fatal Inheritance

The potentially fatal consequences of these inherited behaviour patterns relate specifically to the one animal species, Homo sapiens. Having evolved a conscious self-awareness, and the ability to make much of nature its servant, mankind is now endeavouring to exempt itself from the evolutionary process of adaptation to environment change. In nature, only those individuals with suitable anatomical, physiological or behavioural qualities best suited to the prevailing environmental circumstances survive, while those less well suited individuals do not. A current endeavour of mankind, by contrast to the natural process of selection, is to eliminate all the major causes of untimely deaths. Without deliberate population limitation this is an impossible endeavour, unless the food supply can be continuously increased, and at an ever increasing rate. If universal survival to maturity could be achieved, and all were then free to reproduce without restraint, a consequence would be a gradual lowering of the suitability of the species to survive without artificial support processes. In fact, selection of the fittest to survive is too powerful a process to be substantially subdued, and despite the human endeavours to subdue it, is operating continuously in one way or another. Such 'scourges' as malaria and tuberculosis continue to differentiate between those with adequate resistance to the infection, who survive, and those without it, who may not survive. Surely the epidemics of bubonic plague in the fifteenth century and of influenza in 1918 were operations of natural selection which determined survival or non-survival on the basis of relative abilities to resist that particular environmental challenge.

Subsequent reproduction, and therefore genome inheritance, was undoubtedly affected by this natural selection. This may have contributed to the eventual extinction of those epidemics, and most likely rendered subsequent generations more resistant to those particular challenges, for a while at least. There would, of course, be great benefit to individual lifetimes if malaria, tuberculosis, and now AIDS, could be eradicated by medical and scientific endeavours. This, however, could lower the extent of natural resistance to these diseases, and render communities ever more dependent upon progressive medical intervention to sustain resistance. If, in any circumstances, that protection should become unavailable, epidemic outbreaks of those diseases would have devastating consequences, because of the reduced level of natural immunity.

On several counts, then, it could be utterly fallacious to

presume that the human species generally would benefit in a lasting way from the further mastery of nature that it relentlessly seeks to achieve. This brings me right back to the concern of some of my erstwhile colleagues in the 1940s that the introduction of the antibiotics to control many infections, and of insecticides to wipe out the malaria-transmitting mosquito, would fail as lasting benefits if the lives of those 'saved' by these developments in medicine and public health could not then be sustained. Lasting benefit would be only for those whose lives could remain unaffected by consequential food shortages. For medical advances to be universally applicable, there has to be a coincidental and substantial increase in food production to accommodate all those 'saved' by the therapy from early deaths. Furthermore, since more survivors to adulthood results in more mating couples, and thereby an increasing birth rate, food production then has to rise more or less exponentially for ever afterwards. For many reasons touched upon earlier in this text, there is no possibility that food production could be continuously increased to feed a continuously increasing human population for more than a relatively brief period. Thus we are all fooling ourselves when we assume that there is no price to pay for endeavouring to opt out of the processes of survival of the fittest in an intensely competitive total environment.

As this section was being written, a leader article in the then current issue of *New Scientist* stated that 'Every one wants to save as many lives as they can'. The sentiment is fine, but it is sadly remote from the reality of what is possible. The consequence of the continuing endeavours to curb every major cause of early human death could only be a shift in the cause of premature deaths from treatable diseases to the untreatable conditions of starvation and its collateral consequences. As the food shortage increases, there will then be an increased level of belligerency.

The rise in the human population that occurred in the second half of the twentieth century is explicable only by the increase in food production during that time. That does not mean that it has been possible to sustain every life saved by modern medicine. Almost certainly the increasing birth rate has stayed ahead of the increasing agricultural productivity and, as has always been the case, hunger and the premature death of some proportion of the human population has continued to be the final determinant of population size. Obviously, because of the finite nature of everything on Earth, food production cannot be increased continuously for ever. Eventually efforts to produce ever more food to stave off a rising incidence of premature deaths will come to a halt, and will then most probably start to decline. There will be no refuge when that occurs. A population crash will be upon us, and the magnitude of the ensuing horror will be of our own making. We will have believed for too long that with our cleverness in forcing nature to do our bidding, the human species could sustain itself for ever on its own terms, rather than on those of unmanaged nature.

Clearly it is not the three basic behavioural inheritances themselves, but the influence upon them of the development of the level of human consciousness that has enabled Homo sapiens to control and change the material and the nature of its environment, always for its own immediate benefit. This, it seems, has led mankind into the biological cul-de-sac of trying to keep ever more people alive by any and every means that it can master. If we continue to breed in excess of survivability, endeavours to keep ever more of us alive, and exercise unbridled belligerency to protect our own interests at anyone else's expense, ultimate disaster in inevitable. This is because the widespread hunger when attempts to further increase food supplies fail, will compel us to fight each other for possession of what food there is. As Adolf Hitler pointed out in *Mein Kampf*, though not in these precise terms, no one voluntarily dies of starvation, so when there is bread to be stolen one endeavours to steal it. Whenever harvests begin to fail, conflicts always follow.

War, however, is no longer what it used to be. They were always bitter and bloody affairs, fought with every means available until one contestant was victorious, and the other was defeated and, perhaps, totally destroyed. Now the military weaponry available to the belligerents is of such destructive capability that it is described in multiples of total annihilation, or 'overkill'. History shows us that when the circumstances are desperate enough, the adversaries will employ every means they have to avoid defeat. When two adversaries both possess overkill' capability, the 'first strike' strategy may then be imperative for there to be any chance of victory, and the most effective weaponry at their disposal will be used. The possible, and now likely, consequence of that could be the annihilation of both parties to the quarrel, and maybe of many more not directly involved in the conflict.

The only hope of avoiding this risk of destruction of a whole civilisation, and thereby allowing the continuation of the dominance of Homo sapiens amongst living things, is to use the human intellect to call our behavioural inheritances to order. Many things need to be done to stabilise the relations between the human overlord and the environment which it is now sorely abusing. The most imperative of all is that of keeping the human population of the world at the level at which all can be fed indefinitely. Only then, will there be no need for hunger-induced human conflicts. If we choose not to do so, either our own acts of belligerency, or the normal course of nature, will be the population controller. By one way or the other the population size will be reduced to whatever level the food supply can then sustain. Either of those alternatives will be massively painful, but neither need occur if we are as intelligent as we think we are, and can use our intelligence to take command of our own destiny.

The sophisticated lifestyles that many of us are able to enjoy today are all products of application of science to the exploitation or use of various components of the natural environment. Science, or knowledge (*scio* (L) = I know), is the product of the application of an exceptional development of the human central nervous system, which has enabled it to enquire methodically about all that surrounds it. The paradox of this is that the development of human brainpower which has afforded us this ability to investigate, understand and exploit components of the environment, has also enabled us to create the means of destroying everything that human brainpower has achieved – and perhaps ourselves as well.

Over thousands of years this organised and directed curiosity led us, slowly but progressively, to advance the understanding of our total environment, and to the use of that knowledge to improve the living conditions of mankind. In the course of the last 500 years this progression has moved forward at an constantly increasing pace, and with it, so have the advances in industry, agriculture and medicine. Now, it seems, we can take and mould the environment more or less as we wish, and all for the benefit – and glory – of mankind. It is this acquired mastery, particularly over food production, that has been the cause of the rapid and progressive increase in the human population. Until the time of the industrial revolution mankind had caused little or no lasting environmental damage. The human population rise at the time of, and since, the industrial revolution, and the changes in human activities and lifestyles are now altering the environment to an alarming degree, and not now in ways that are likely to be of enduring benefit to mankind.

In particular, mankind has learned how to determine which plants shall grow in abundance and where, and which animals shall be allowed to coexist with us, in order to produce food for human consumption. This has resulted in an uncontrolled feedforward/feed backward action: more food allows the survival of more people, and more people create an even greater demand on food production. Considering the finite nature of our planet-home, it is a matter of common sense that this upward spiralling of food production, population sizes and the raping of the Earth's crust cannot continue indefinitely. At some time this expansion of the Earth's resources will have to cease. The most likely first evidence of this will be harvest failures. These may be because of the exhaustion of the soil per se, the failures of water supplies for irrigation, or the loss of fertile coastal and delta lands as global warming causes the sea level to rise. Inadequate supplies of potable water for human consumption may compound the disaster. Such an occurrence would inevitably lead to a human population crash – with or without the assistance of human conflicts over possession of what necessities of life remain available, but most likely with that assistance.

This increasingly dangerous situation in which we are now placed relates ultimately to the sheer mass of humanity, with each member now wanting, expecting, demanding and seeking a 'place in the sun'. The demand for agriculture expansion has been spurred by the labour demands of the industrial applications of knowledge, and the success of the application of science to medicine and public health to the lengthening of the mean life expectancy. Thus the present situation is not so much the consequence of three inherited behavioural features themselves, as of their influences within the context of the capabilities of the extraordinary development of the human central nervous system.

The Emergence of Human Consciousness

It is pertinent to consider how the central nervous system of Homo sapiens came to be of a quite different order of capability than those of other extant primates, which have been evolving in hostile environments for just as long. Many believe that the explanation is non-biological and that the human mind, if not the brain, was a separate supernatural endowment. Homo sapiens had evolved, however, long before Paul metamorphosed the strictly tribal Jewish god, Yahweh, into the universal pan-tribal deity which is now much revered in one way or another. There is historical awareness of at least 2,500 gods, each of which has been fervently believed in and worshipped by one human group or another, at one time or another (see Jordan, 1992). Most of them have died and are now forgotten, and there is no discernible reason why any one contemporary set of beliefs in a supernatural deity should be considered any more likely to be true than any other at any time. Not only is there no positive evidence in support of any of these supernatural hypotheses, but also contemporary theologians are distinctly vague about when it is supposed the distinction between man and other animals occurred, and by the will of which divinity. If it occurred, it was certainly long before there was any concept of one universal deity. Now that the general principles of evolution are well supported by a vast body of evidence, there can be few well-versed biologists who would not wish to have a biological explanation for human brainpower, stated in terms of the selection of the fittest to survive in natural, often hostile and continuously changing environments.

Nothing is provable beyond dispute, but it is seemingly reasonable to believe that the human brain, and the exceptionally large range of uses to which it can be put, must have come about by evolutionary adaptation to prevailing environmental circumstances. Right up to the time when Homo sapiens could create its own local protected environments, survival depended on the ability to compete successfully with other predators and food-gathering competitors. Other species had to do the same, and most still have to, so commonly experienced environmental challenges cannot account for the particular evolution of human brainpower. This, it is believed, was first employed in the development of instruments, tactics and strategies of attack and defence, which enhanced the species competence in hunting and in war.

A likely – perhaps *the* most likely – explanation is that the progenitors of Homo sapiens needed to compete aggressively for the control of territory, access to food, and for mating privileges, not only with other species of hunters and gatherers, but also with other packs or tribes of its own species. Many other extant animal species, and not only other primates, also engage in both interspecies and intraspecies struggles for dominance and food. Perhaps, as well as the three basic inherited behavioural features discussed above, prehuman and human tribes became increasingly ruthless in their intra-species conflicts, with an increasing tendency to eliminate the vanquished enemy. Thus the selection would be of the individuals best fitted to win in genocidal tribal warfare. As this line of selection continued there could have been ever more dependence on guile and weaponry rather than upon physical strength alone. In turn, such mastery of weapons and warfare would have been dependent upon the progressive development intellectual prowess and, therefore, of the central nervous system. What, then, was being selected every time one party annihilated another and achieved local monopoly of parenthood, could have been the ability to outwit others in the weaponry and the tactics of belligerency.

If the enhanced performance of the human brain was selected in part at least, because it facilitated victory in intertribal conflicts, it becomes understandable not only that the three basic behavioural features of animals have remained powerful human inheritances, but also that Homo sapiens so readily resorts to warfare when personal or tribal interests are threatened. All of the elastic capabilities of human consciousness, and its use to explore and understand the environment, can be considered as divergent applications of these features of the human brain and consciousness. The pursuit of self-interest, irrespective of the consequences to others, is practised universally, and can be seen to be operating in many subtle and less than subtle ways. The Achilles heel of democracy, for example, is that most individuals vote for what seems to be best for them at that time, and not what would be best for all either now or in the future. It is for the aggressive defence of the interests of states, and in obtaining and maintaining the supplies of food and other needs of modern lifestyles, that nations strive to develop the means to defeat enemies and potential enemies. The destructive power of modern weaponry is a consequence of this, and is now a potential threat to us all.

There is not much that can now be done to undo the influences that human consciousness exerts on the three basic behavioural inheritances, particularly in attack and defence as self-interest requires. Together they constitute the 'new' behavioural inheritance package, which enables Homo sapiens to dominate almost all else of the living world. If Homo sapiens continue on this course of ruthless and aggressive self-interest, it now seems more likely than not that the concerted influence of consciousness and instinct upon human behaviour will lead to eventual disaster. This could all but end the human hegemony. Intertribal and inter-theological warring is where the ultimate danger lies. If we continue to exercise no positive control over human population sizes, and we therefore have to rely on our ability to continuously increase agricultural productivity, and if personal and tribal interests and conflicting theological dogmas remain our dominant considerations, the scene is set. With population sizes ultimately determined, as always, by the food supply, and with the certainty that food production will reach a zenith, and then most probably will decline, the ensuing hunger will result in food wars. In that circumstance the annihilation of the vanquished side to reduce the number of competitors for a dwindling food supply will be the only rational action. When such brutal exercises in population control have reduced the human population to below the level at which all can be fed, the population will then start to rise again. Hunger will then reappear and soon a population crash will recur. The populations of other species cycle in this way, and Homo sapiens is not immune to this sequence of events. It just has to occur once food production can no longer be expanded to accommodate a rising population. The only difference is that Homo sapiens, by warfare and genocide, can, and probably will, expedite the population decline. What now spoils this prediction of a recurring cycle of population growth and brutal population collapse, is mankind's refinement of the means of conducting war and genocide. These are now of such potentially destructive power that their use could, indeed, overkill to the extent that we will undo all that mankind has achieved, and which has been given the dubiously appropriate name of 'civilisation', which once meant *good citizenship*.

If, by some extraordinary exercise of mind over matter, we could reach a species-wide agreement to forego all our modern means of mass destruction, would that put us back on course for species longevity? No, not by itself! We have travelled too far along the road of environmental exploitations for a will for peace alone to be an effective medicine. It could avoid for a while longer the sudden end of Homo sapiens as the super-animal, but it could not prevent the animal-like population cycling once food production has reached its zenith. The need to compete for possession of what food there is, would surely place any peace-pact under tremendous strain. Any means of achieving pacification before the weapons of mass destruction do their worst is, however, worthy of consideration. It could allow us a little time in which to act, and for those who can do so, to think to good purpose.

A GM Escape Route?

There could be no natural process of selection of a breed of non-aggressive Homo sapiens because the pacified strain would be eliminated long before it could have become the dominant one. On the contrary it would seem that intraspecific belligerency has become intensified in humans, while the instincts to procreate excessively, and to be primarily concerned with self and self-preservation, have surely remained undiluted. Thus we are, by nature, a threat not only to all other competing species, but also to competitors within our own species. When interests conflict, this intraspecific intolerance is much greater in humans than in our nearest extant primate relatives and is now disastrously so.

Eugenics (= good breeding), which is a term coined by Francis Galton in 1883, is the study of the ways of managing the positive selection of desirable physical and mental qualities of human beings. Although quickly condemned on moral and ethical grounds by clergy and laymen alike, its practical application is always with us. It was put into practice by the Nazis in the 1930s, in an attempt to fulfil the dream of a genetically pure master race, freed of what was perceived to be the unwanted features of a co-existing minority tribe. There was positive genetic selection both by the arranged matings of archetype Aryan nationals, and by the genocide of the unwanted non-Aryan citizens. Sadly, the identification of the victims was often rendered easier by their characteristic facial features, and aided by the tribal practice of male circumcision. The somewhat distinctive facial features exist because the 'offending' tribe itself has long practised the eugenic custom of intratribal marriage, to preserve tribal integrity.

In retrospect it was unfortunate that the eugenicist Karl Pearson had proclaimed, in 1919, 'History shows me one way, and one way only, in which a state of high civilization has been produced, namely, the struggle of race with race, and the survival of the mentally fitter race.' There could be an element of truth in that utterance in praise of nationalism, and the apparently exceptional intellectual quality of many Jews could have that basis. Pearson's statement might, however, be interpreted as supportive of a less civilised nationalism with prowess in aggression, and the elimination of intertribal competition, as the basis of the fitness to survive and flourish. It was only shortly after Pearson's proclamation that Adolf Hitler formulated his belief in the supremacy of a master race (his, of course), and expressed it in his diatribe, *Mein Kampf.* So far as I know there is no evidence that

Hitler's intense racist philosophy and policies were encouraged directly by Pearson's utterances, but according to Black (2004) the writings and activities of eugenicists in the USA were well studied by Hitler in the 1920s, and these almost certainly did strengthened his willingness to pursue a policy of annihilation of 'undesirable' persons in order to establish a pure and healthy Aryan race.

Positive genetic selection was later introduced much more moderately in Singapore in 1986, in the form of preferential economic benefits for female university graduates when they produce offspring. The intention here was to raise the intellectual capabilities of the Singapore citizenship. The ingrained self-interest of Homo sapiens and the penchant for tribal cohesion and affinity probably guarantees that attempts will continue to be made to gain personal or tribal benefit from selective breeding. By such means the so-called royal families of Europe consolidated their collective dominance and power. It would seem, from the remnants of that dynasty, however, that they noticeably failed to concentrate and strengthen any intellectual prowess. Hopefully, future exercises in eugenics will not include the mass extermination practised by the Nazis. However, as was discerned by Charles Darwin, mass extermination of those unfitted to survive in any prevailing environmental circumstance is an essential part of the natural processes of selection of the fittest to survive.

The latest major accomplishment of mankind's organised and directed curiosity is the deciphering and the reading of the genetic 'instruction book' for the construction and maintenance of living systems – the genetic code. Efforts are now being made to apply this knowledge to the elimination of genetic defects, which are expressed phenotypically as debilitating functional abnormalities. Like all else of medical research and medical practice, this is a humane endeavour pursued with the best intentions of reducing suffering. Most likely, however, there is a downside to these advances. As every livestock farmer knows, the maintenance of a healthy herd or flock depends on the culling of those animals which, if used for breeding, would have financially disastrous consequences. The animal breeder's concern is the market value of the product, but this can apply also to human beings in terms of their employability, and in other ways as well.

The current demand by citizens of the so-called 'developed countries' is for 100% survival from birth through to maturity, and beyond; and for the right of all to reproduce. Since these demands are consistent with the protective instincts of parent, its collective expression would therefore be difficult to curb. If achieved, however, and widely applied, this would put an end to the process of natural selection, with the consequent retention and spread of defective or inadequate genetic material. With this there would most likely be the progressive weakening of the survivability of many individuals if they were ever removed from the protective environments of the man-shaped societies that provide the continuous benefits of medicine and other life supports. Genetic engineering and pre-birth genetic selection could, it can be claimed, reduce the rate of genetic deterioration in a '100% survival' society.

Such processes to eliminate phenotypic abnormalities, however, are unlikely ever to become as universally applicable as are the other processes by which the childbirth mortality can be minimised. Furthermore, such genetic selection to eliminate particular risks may leave other less life-threatening defects to be passed on by reproduction. Thus, even ignoring the increasing problem of how to feed all the 'saved' lives, the achievement of the ideal of 100% survival ideal would, by cancelling out the early elimination of those with genetic defects, place mankind in ever increasing jeopardy. This reduced survivability could then influence the consequences of a challenge by another life form such as a pathogenic virus or micro-organism, or by a man-induced environmental change. There could also be a slow but progressive lowering of the level of human intelligence which could also lower the fitness of the species to survive. No doubt, in time, engineered genetic modifications will reduce the chances of inherited phenotypic disorders, and the pains they cause to both parents and the afflicted offspring. The sheer logistics of applying such benefits to more than a favoured minority of the human population of the world, however, will surely negate its effectiveness as a means of making every matured individual fit enough to reproduce.

Taking into account all the positive and negative effects of selective breeding and deliberately engineered genetic modifications, both immediately and eventually, they would be better left alone than carried too far. This is a 'soul-searching' moral dilemma, for carefully considered limited applications of genetic manipulation in a strictly medical context would be of undoubted immediate benefit to a fortunate minority with access to it.

An immediate threat to the future of Homo sapiens lies in the extension of more general medical developments that can eliminate major causes of early death, and which are universally applicable. This is not because they will have greater impact per se than that of the introduction of vaccination in the eighteenth century or of antibiotics in the twentieth century, but because it will now be increasingly difficult to provide the additional food required for the 'saved lives'. By increasing the food shortage, and increasing the extent of the hunger and hunger-induced premature deaths, medicine could itself undo all the intended good of medical research and application.

Even if this scenario should become generally recognised as the likely direction of human progress, it is unlikely to temper the current efforts to achieve universalise survival from conception to old age, and then to extend life expectancy yet further. This is because we are genetically conditioned to be far more interested in our own lifetimes and our own survival prospects than in the fate of future generations beyond those of our own children. Now, though, with the extended life expectancy of the more fortunate of us, the parental protective instinct has become extended to the next generation or two of kinsfolk which we may survive for long enough to know. Beyond that limited extension, however, there is negligible concern for the well-being of future generations.

The most worrisome component of the behavioural inheritance is that of belligerency, now that it could be utterly disastrous. Thus it might seem attractive to identity the gene or genes which dictate our basic behaviour patterns and to make attempts by genetic modification, to produce a less self-centred and less aggressive version of Homo sapiens that will live happily and at peace with all others of its own species. That sounds idyllic but, as already explained, it would not work if only because while still in the minority in a belligerent world, these genetically modified Homo sapiens would lack the competitive edge and would most likely be eliminated.

Since there can be no universal process of genetic modification or selection by which the more troublesome behavioural traits of humans could be are bred out, the only other way to regain the prospect of a future for Homo sapiens, is to strive for worldwide acceptance of the need to control the size of the human population, and thus reduce the need for war in the struggle for survival.

The Prospect of Keeping Human Populations Within Feedable Limits

Those not wishful of any restraint upon sexual freedom in order to keep populations at feedable levels can often be heard to argue that there is food enough for the six billion extant human beings, and that the only cause of hunger is the inequitable distribution of world food production. It is surely self-evident that since that number of humans exist, there is food enough at present to keep that number alive, and that were it to be equitably distributed, hunger would be less in evidence than it is now. That comforting truism, however, ignores the fact that with massive excessive procreation in many parts of the world, human populations are being kept at their present levels by the premature deaths of the 'surplus' progeny. The hunger in the world today is not solely attributable to the inequitable distribution of food, although that is a substantial factor. Even if that were the sole factor, however, the well-fed societies are mostly in states that are democratically ruled, and their electorates would be as strongly opposed to any enforced equitable distribution of food, which would reduce their own living standards, as they would be to any enforced restraint on their freedom to reproduce according to their own desires.

Since the earliest times of land management, food production in excess of the needs of the farmers and their families has been a marketable product. By that means of distribution only those with sufficient purchasing power could, and still can, obtain all they need, while those without the purchasing power go hungry or survive on charity or by theft. The provision of medicine is also a largely commercial activity, and even where it is 'free at the point of delivery' (i.e. prepaid for through taxation) its lasting benefit remains dependent upon the availability of food, and that depends on the ability to purchase it. The benefits of purchasing power operate at tribal or national levels as well as that of the individual, and it is the affluent societies that can import all the food needed to keep their supermarkets well stocked, even when the population greatly exceeds the number which it own level of food production could sustain. The commercial food importers are unlikely to be greatly concerned about any adverse effects the transactions may have upon the communities that are exporting the food. In some instances the exported food is not truly surplus to the local needs of the country producing it. The food is being exported only to gain the foreign currency needed for the purchase of other things such as arms for defence against external or internal threats, or to service debts to foreign bankers. Even where the exportation of food is genuinely surplus to the needs of the exporting state, the exportation may not be to those countries in greatest need of that surplus, but instead to those best able to pay the market price for it. It is also unlikely that this commercial basis for food distribution could be varied. That is because it has been a tradable commodity almost from the dawn of agricultural history. It is also because political systems intended to achieve distribution of food on the basis of need rather than purchasing power, have never worked as intended. Individual and corporate self-interest soon results in ways to wreck such attempts, and re-establish personal benefit.

Despite the assertion that populations always expand as far as the food supply will allow, and are then held at that maximal level by premature deaths, it is interesting and noteworthy that not all affluent populations do so, even when they produce, or can import, enough food to allow population growth. This deviation from the basic biological tendency is mostly the consequence of voluntary birth control. This is not, however, in order to spare the world from the disaster of overpopulation, but to maximise the personal benefits of affluence. With smaller families parental responsibilities can then be adequately fulfilled without sacrificing the hedonistic lifestyles which economic privilege allows. Furthermore, when there are only two or three children to be succoured each one can be given educational and other social advantages calculated to improve their prospects in the highly competitive environments in which their lives will be spent. This shift in the preferred family size is not because human natural instincts have been subdued. It is a social adaptation based on the inherited instinct to succour one's own progeny in whatever way is best suited to the prevailing environmental circumstances. Sexual restraint is no longer necessary for that achievement.

The preference for smaller families than the unimpeded exercise of conjugal rights would otherwise create is not now restricted to the more affluent communities. In some considerably less affluent ones which, until quite recently, had alarmingly high birth rates, a similar restriction in family size is becoming evident. One reason for this is believed to stem from the vast improvements in paediatric medicine and childcare, which has improved the prospects of survival of progeny into adulthood. Without reproductive restraint this increased survival rate could lead to families being too large to be adequately supported by the family income. Another reported influence on family size is the improved status of women. When the female partner has some say in the frequency of pregnancy many women, it seems, then choose to have only two or three children, as do many European and North American women. This is in their own interest as well as that of the family unit.

Elsewhere the spectre of unmanageable increases in population, and resultant starvation on massive scales, has caused governments to actively encourage birth control. The government of at least one country has resorted to statutory control over family size. There is some evidence, however, that such enforcement can give rise to an increase in infanticide as an alternative to paying the penalty for non-adherence to the law.

Evidently, then, in appropriate economic and/or social contexts, population control can be elective, and particularly so when it is recognised by mated pairs to be in the best interests of themselves and their progeny. Where such limitation is for the wider benefit of societies rather than for individual families, voluntary birth control may be less readily achievable. Thus to protect the species both now and in the future, strong persuasion or enforcement may be necessary. Unfortunately, it is in the regions of the world where the need for population control is greatest, that doctrinal instructions forbidding birth control remains most influential.

As has been stated already, the fact that there are 6,000 million extant human beings is proof that that number of human beings can be sustained, at least at a marginal level of adequacy. That crude equation between population and food supply leaves unstated why the equation exists. It is not that at every social level, and everywhere, every newborn child could be adequately fed with an equal chance of a full life. The current world population is what it is because premature deaths of the underfed produce that result. It is also true that if affluent and unnecessarily well-fed sections of the world societies, were to behave uncharacteristically and support an equitable distribution of food worldwide, the pain and hunger could be lessened for a while.

That, however, is an academic consideration, and not only because of the inherent human nature by which self-consideration and self-preservation always predominates. The relief that an equitable food distribution would allow would be brief. That is because a fall in the incidence of premature death would result in an increased number of mated couples a few years later, and thereby result in an increase in the birth rate. Thus world population would soon rise again to that extent at which population control is again affected by the occurrence of premature deaths. Without deliberate birth control there is no way to escape from natural population control by the premature deaths of the unfeedable surplus. Further expansions of the food supply could cause only brief relief unless a continuously expansion of agriculture can be sustained throughout the foreseeable future. This, again, is because every increase in food production facilitates a further increase in world population. Clearly, however, a continuously increasing production of food throughout the foreseeable future is an unrealisable aspiration. Indeed, there can be no guarantee that even the present agricultural output can be maintained indefinitely. Ultimately there must be a limit to whatever increase is yet possible. Eventually soil exhaustion, or the shortage of water for irrigation, will cause food production to plummet, and then the full horror of a human population crash will be upon us. As hunger spreads, individuals and communities will become increasingly concerned to put their own nutritional needs above those of all others. This will give rise to conflicts of unparalleled magnitude which will abate only when human populations have been reduced to whatever level the reduced supply of food can then sustain.

We may, or may not, be already close to the limit of agricultural possibilities. There are signs that the first green revolution, based on land clearance, plant breeding, mineral soil enrichment, irrigation, and selective herbicides, insecticides and fungicides, is now nearing its zenith. Higher mineral applications to the soil no longer result in economic increases in crops. Subterranean aquifers, used for irrigation and by industries and homes, are becoming exhausted and/or polluted. Salt deposits on topsoils as a result of irrigation are reducing productivity. It is apparent, then, that a second 'green revolution' is urgently necessary if a levelling out of, and a possible fall in, food production is to be averted. The only substantial candidate for this is the genetic modification of food-yielding plants, so that they can thrive in semi-arid and/or salt-damaged soils, have resistance to plant diseases, and/or be unattractive to competing herbivores. Given adequate research funding, there is still the possibility of delaying a pending human population crash, although any increase in food production will not, by itself, permanently eliminate that threat of a human population crash.

The funding of the need to maximise the effectiveness of a second green revolution would be better made and controlled by governmental or intergovernmental agencies, than by commercial enterprises with hidden agenda of interest only to their shareholders. It must be understood, however, that unless a second green revolution is accompanied by an adequate level of population control, it can only buy time, and cannot achieved a lasting solution to this pending human problem. Today, then, agricultural research is a vital scientific endeavour, but even more important than agricultural research, is the acceptance of the need for worldwide population control.

The current ill-reasoned negative attitude towards the development of genetically altered food-producing plants, and the current increasing preference for the so-called 'organic' farm produce, are not helpful. There is scope for cheating in 'organic' farming, for additional organic matter is needed to sustain the productivity of the soil. Since this cannot come from other 'organic' farmland, it is likely to be obtained from where the farming is 'non-organic'. The supplier is then compelled to apply even more mineral fertilisers to his own land in order to sustain his own crop yields. Furthermore, the yield obtainable by 'organic' farming is always, or almost always, far less than that of non-organically-farmed land. Going 'organic' is then a luxury cult for an already over-indulged section of society, but is a negative influence on worldwide food production.

As for genetically modified (GM) crops, there is the risk that harm could be done if there were to be some untoward consequence of a modification calculated to be wholly beneficial. This is much as a medicine of proven clinical benefit may be found to have adverse side effects. There is also reason to suspect that commercially run GM research establishments cannot be trusted to be motivated only by what would be most beneficial to humanity at large. The harmful consequences of not endeavouring to maximise agricultural productivity, however, will almost certainly be far greater than the consequences of a GM mishap. Resistance to the marketing of GM food products until there has been adequate time and opportunity to evaluate the risks, however, is reasonable. The near-panic in the attitudes of many individuals to GM crops, based on the premise that the safe guarding of ones own health takes precedence over that of mankind at large, is less laudable.

Saving the Children

From what has been written above about populations and their food supplies, it is evident that there is no way by which every child brought into the world could be sustained into maturity, and every adult life then substantially extended, without some degree of birth control. As Thomas Malthus learned to his discomfort, it is difficult to discuss the implications of that assertion in a rational and well-intended way without creating the impression that one is indifferent to the agonies of starving children. Most of us, it seems, feel more compelled to offer what protection we can to young children – irrespective of ethnic, religious or tribal distinctions – than to adults who can be perceived as being different from ourselves. This extended parental concern is essentially an instinctive pattern of behaviour which is not an exclusively human characteristic, being also evident in some other mammalian species. It is there, presumably, because it maximises the chances of the survival of the progeny, and, no doubt, this has played a crucial role in evolutionary progressions.

Thus even when the impossibility of shielding every infant from the agonies and terminal consequence of hunger is recognised, the majority of us remain immediately responsive to those television appeals which bring the suffering of starving children right into our living rooms. Thus it may seem improper and pointless to question the long-term effectiveness of bringing aid to hungry populations generally, and to hungry children particularly. When a famine results from an exceptional meteorological circumstance that is unlikely to persist over years, such temporary relief may be sufficient to avert a disaster. Where, however, there is a chronic and growing imbalance between population size and the available food supply, short-duration aid, by itself, is more a palliative than a cure. Unless the aid can then be sustained over years, or unless concurrent actions are taken both to improve local food production and to moderate the rate of population growth, it is unlikely to be as remedial as the donors hope. A high rate of infant mortality will only be postponed for a while by emergency aid, for if the saved infants survive into adulthood, a rise in the number of mating couples will eventually recreate the famine conditions. Infant mortality will then occur on an even greater scale.

This is precisely the situation discerned by Thomas Malthus two hundred years ago, and no doubt he then wished that what his reasoning compelled him to say could be disproved. There was then, as now, no lack of denigrators of the Malthusian thesis, but not on substantial and logical grounds. There has never been an intellectually convincing refutation, nor can there be. The fact of the matter is that without deliberate reproductive restraint the human species, like virtually all other animal species, will breed in excess of the number that could achieve maturity. So long as the available food supply determines population size, by the natural means of population adjustment, infant mortality is a component of the controlling mechanism. No matter what one is told to believe, or one chooses to belief, to the contrary, there is no evidence of an automatic protection of the human species from this natural estate save that of our latent intellectual ability to sustain a balance between populations and their food supplies by the unnatural but humane way of wilful birth control. That is surely preferable to the natural but inhumane way of premature deaths from starvation.

This is an uncomfortable conclusion, and must leave many of us in a terrible quandary. To charge a supernatural deity with the responsibility of 'supplying the wants of others' in the 'grace' before one's own substantial meal, sounds to the unindoctrinated humanitarian like a pathetic avoidance of human responsibility. Of course, once the children exist one cannot knowingly and wilfully leave them to suffer hunger and early deaths if there are the means to prevent it. The fact of the matter, however, is that famine crises are now occurring with increasing frequency and severity. Already it is quite impossible to reach out to every starving child, or even just those that we come to know about through media reports. Already there is some indication of a sense of helplessness and weariness amongst those who want to help, but cannot do so, or cannot do so adequately, every time an appeal is launched. Already it is foreseeable that the time will come when the market demand for exportable food supplies will leave nothing in the granaries of the world for charitable distribution.

Sooner or later the realities of an increasingly sad and dangerous situation will compel mankind to think beyond the comforting mythologies of a caring deity that, if prevailed upon, will 'supply the wants of others'. The underlying cause of hunger and premature death is the inherited urge to reproduce in excess of supportability. The only possible lasting solution is birth control by one means or another.

I wanted to avoid the need to write this section of my thesis, in which honest analysis and emotional involvement are clearly at war with each other. Still less have I wanted to observe that the innocence of infancy is so soon lost, once the active involvement in the struggle for personal survival begins. Of the trinity of the causes of war – hunger, tribalism and theology – hunger is the prime one, although the need for conflict is readily aided and abetted by tribal antagonisms and by differing supernaturalist dogmas. All three, alas, are serious enough at times to end in genocide, but it is hunger that is the most genocidal. When one wins the battle for land rights, the annihilation of the vanquished is the only sure way of gaining vacant possession. The encouragement and facilitation of population growth by giving alms can, as Malthus concluded, cause future suffering on a greater scale than that which alms were originally intended to alleviate. Thus those whose decent endeavours is to 'save the children' might well ask themselves 'Save for what?'. Is it for an even greater degree of suffering tomorrow; for ever more ruthless human conflicts, or to strive to reach an unreachable Utopia?

I now know the pain and the dilemma that greatly troubled Thomas Malthus, and spoiled his relationships with his fellow men, both then and now. I have no doubt that as a clergyman he found no joy in stating what his intellectual integrity and concern for human suffering compelled because it seemed to him to be a sad truth. Of course, every effort must be made to avoid suffering. That remedy, however, will never be enough to achieve that goal without a wilful limitation upon the occurrence of birth. Thus there is no cowardice or hypocrisy in my continuing willingness to contribute to charities which seek to provide relief from hunger, but I earnestly wish that the root cause of much of the hunger was now being addressed with as much eagerness and concern as is being directed to the attempts to give immediate relief of that suffering.

The Quest for Immortality

There will be life on Earth, of one sort or another, for as long as sufficient solar radiation falls upon the Earth's surfaces to support it. No extant species, however, carries any guarantee of such duration, and no individual unit of life can, at the present time at least, remain extant for more than a quite brief period. Life, then, is a successional phenomenon, being passed on by asexual or sexual reproduction, from one biological structure to a succeeding one. With the advent of consciousness, which is evidently more well developed in humans than in other species, Homo sapiens is able to reflect on the past and contemplate the future. Our awareness of the eventual inevitability of death makes the notion of a life everlasting an attractive proposition. Thus throughout the recorded history of mankind the promise of an afterlife has been a readily saleable philosophical commodity, which people have been anxious to believe in and to qualify for.

Despite the popularly received promises of an eternity far grander than anything ever experienced during a lifetime on Earth, most of us are anxious to avoid a premature death. It is now being mooted that biological knowledge is becoming so complete that it may be possible to postpone death indefinitely. Indeed, Michael Rose of the University of California is reported (*New Scientist,* No. 2309, 2001) to be confident that the ability to escape death already exists. He believes that there are already people around who could live for ever, provided they can avoid life-threatening accidents and infections at all times in the future. This was described in the *New Scientist* as a 'new optimism', but whether one should greet the prospects with optimism or pessimism is at least arguable.

When the size of a population is unchanging over any length of time, as it must be if the food supply is unchanging, birth rates and death rates must be in balance. Populations can be increased briefly by increases in the birth rate, or when the mortality rate is reduced at one or the other extremes of a lifetime by virtue of medical intervention. Such population growth cannot be sustained, however, if the food needed to support a larger population is not forthcoming. An immediate effect of an increase in the life expectancy of adults is to reduce the food available for new arrivals. Any temporary imbalance between births and deaths due to death avoidance by adults is therefore likely to increase the incidence of infant mortality. From these considerations, it is evident that the searched-for elixir of life could not be applied worldwide. If it should become possible to extend lifetimes indefinitely, this presumed privilege would have to be confined to only a relatively small number of humans. The only alternative to such selection for longevity would be the limitation of procreation to that limited extent needed to replace accidental and incidental losses of life. Birth control would have to be imposed, and if power should fall into the hands of a dictator whose own natural death could no longer be anticipated enthusiastically, this perpetual ruler would, no doubt, decree whose lives would be extended indefinitely, and whose would be brought to an early end. That dictator could, and probably would, also decide who would be allowed to procreate. It would then be only a short step to cloning any needed replacements, and eliminating the reproductive capability of most of the human species.

What is evident is that those biologists whose researches are dedicated to the indefinite postponement of ageing and death are heedless of the social implications of their endeavours. The problems that their success could create surely far outweigh the presumed individual happiness that death avoidance would bring to those allowed to participate in the venture. Medical research, which provides the possibility of a full-length active and healthy lifetime is one thing, although that quest, too, must ultimately be frustrated by the limitation of the food supply. Immortality is another thing. Research to achieve virtual immortality is, then, potentially of such painful consequences that one can only hope that those engaged in that line of research will fail to reach their goal.

In an interview reported in the *New Scientist* (18 October 2003, pp.46–49), under the heading 'I want to live for ever', a reputable biologist expressed her belief that by a combination of dieting and gene-tickling we could all enjoy health, wealth, hordes of children and a greatly extended lifetime. It read like science fiction, and indeed it was. This was not because it may not be possible to find a gene responsible for the ageing process, and to inactivate it, but because the ambition is in defiance of all reason. There is no way by which we could all have extended lives and more progeny. The resources of planet Earth are finite, and so is the number of Homo sapiens that can be housed, fed and watered. To iterate the analogy made earlier in this thesis, one cannot keep more vehicles on the road than there is fuel enough to keep their engines running. If fuel supplies are limited, and the vehicles are made to last longer, fewer new ones can then be commissioned. This imprudent ambition, thinly supported by a veneer of science, stems, no doubt, more from the instinctive wish for life everlasting than from rational thought. It certainly seems unwise to wave this phantom carrot in front of humanity. If one must have such dreams it would be better to stick with the belief in a post-mortem eternity, and to travel hopefully.

The Handicaps of Theologies

That last thought leads to the many theologies of man past and man present. The issues that can be discussed here are not whether any one of them can be any truer than any other, but the practical ones of their contributions to human welfare; and whether they can provide a way through and out of the troubles which humanity is evidently creating for itself. A frank and honest discussion is difficult because theology is a province of rigid notion rather than open, pliable and constructive thought. Dogmas are like blinkers that reduce the field of vision. Once they're fitted, one cannot see more than the field of vision the blinkers allow one to see. Schisms between the mind attuned to science and the mind attuned to theology are inevitable, because of the very different premises upon which considerations are based. This was noted by Francis Bacon (1605) who distinguished between knowledge gained by observation, experimentation and rational analysis, and that based on dogmatic beliefs. Nevertheless, there are aspects of theologies that need to be discussed because they are pertinent to the thesis being presented.

Popular updated theologies, which have evolved to remain credible to and acceptable by an increasingly educated laity, no longer hypothesise a harsh tyrannical egocentric deity with sadistic punishments meted out to those who disobey its edicts while still on Earth or at some later date. The more saleable image now is of a caring and protective deity that only needs to be prayed to earnestly and often, for all to be well. One does not need to be a statistician to know that the lives of those who pray fervently and often are no more free of disappointments, illnesses and disasters than are those that neglect the exercise. When all is not well, as is the case at some time during most lifetimes, the proffered theological explanation is that such painful events are, in some inexplicable way, the will of the deity. The obvious corollary to that explanation is that the presumed deity cannot be relied upon to be caring and protective at all times and in all circumstances. Supernatural favours are as random as chance, and therefore we are all left very much on our own to suffer whatever befalls us.

Logic, however, has little place in theology, and statistics have none whatsoever, and a particular and seriously consequential schism between science and theology is the belief by some supernaturalists that in the particular case of Homo sapiens, there is more to pregnancy than the meeting of an ovum and a sperm: there is the involvement of divine intervention. The corollary of this is that any wilful interference with the process of fertilisation and the subsequent pregnancy is in defiance of that divine will. How, then, it can be that a loveless rape by a predatory male can result in pregnancy is, not surprisingly, left unexplained. Equally problematic and enigmatic to the rational mind is that while some theologians object to interferences with pregnancy and birth, only a very small minority of theologies raise objection to interferences with the natural occurrence of death – which, they are surely bound to aver, is also the deity's will. The reason for this illogical but convenient dichotomy of thought seems to be more biological than theological. The instinct for self-preservation is strong, and it is the endeavour of most animals, including Homo sapiens, to remain amongst the living for as long as possible. A belief that the deliberate interference with a natural causation of death is to frustrate the will of a deity, would not appeal to the priesthood any more than it would to any one else, and would be difficult to sell to the laity. The matter is best 'swept under the carpet'. The universal and instinctive wish for one's life to be sustained for as long as possible, is too strong to be lightly set aside.

It is not only in this regard that religious teachings strongly reflect this instinctive concern for personal survival. The promise of a post-mortem life extension of infinite duration is too attractive a proposition to be lightly refused, particularly because many, if not most, human beings do not find much happiness during their lifetimes. That promise is usually made conditionally upon good behaviour, the definition of which varies between creeds. The condition may be life-long benevolence towards other mortals, irrespective of ethnicity or creed, which is a worthy pursuit whether rewarded or not. Sometimes, however it is strict obedience to sets of rules, which may not make much sense to anyone not indoctrinated in that faith. The believed 'contract' with the deity may allow heinous forms of punishments for disobedience, and authorise acts against perceived heretics which are regarded by humanistic non-adherents to the faith as obscene. Even those theologies that prescribe a code of moral conduct may not apply it very far beyond tribal, theological or class limits. Both in the past and at present, there are instances of encouragement to hate and hound heretics. This 'closed shop' behaviour is surely little more than the expression of instinctive tribal antagonism and belligerency in defence of self, strengthened by doctrinal theological authority.

The now substantial overstocking of our small planet with human beings is, in the final analysis, attributable only to advances in agriculture. It is possible that the current level of agricultural productivity may not be sustainable for very much longer, let alone be greatly expandable. Already it is evident in many quarters of the world that hunger may be on the increase. Quite soon, perhaps, cries for help may be unanswerable for the lack of anything with which to answer. Thus it must be stated openly and honestly that those theologians who argue the sanctity of human life, and thereby oppose birth control are contributors, by their thought control, to much avoidable human suffering, countless premature deaths and bloody and ferocious food wars.

Not withstanding the very solid reasons for concern about the negative influences of some theological doctrines, it must be allowed that at the level of the individual believer, faith in a supernatural protector, and in ultimate eternal salvation, provides for many a sense of comfort in an otherwise comfortless lifetime, and seems, at least, to provide a purpose to life. Sometimes, but only sometimes, it also sustains an ethical modus vivendi. Whether or not there is a real gnostic component to faith what matters to believers and non-believers alike (and we are all non-believers from somebody's point of view!) is whether the moral philosophies invested in a theology succeed in moderating human behaviour for the good. For mankind generally, the worth of a religious doctrine depends not upon whether or not it is true, but upon whether or not it helps its adherents to behave tolerantly and humanely towards all their fellow humans. Many theologies, as actually practised, fail this crucial test. Citations in support of this assertion are not necessary. On most days newspapers provide contemporary evidence of distressing religious bigotry and inhumanity.

If increasing food production allows the world population to continue to increase, it is inevitable that at sometime in the not too distant future this positive interaction between population and food production will cease its upward spiral. Food production must eventually reach a zenith, after which it may decline, a human population crash would then occur. Sooner or later mankind will have to face up to the reality of the situation in which it is placing itself. If it has not already done so, it will be forced to take the only possible action to prevent widespread starvation, uncontrollable pandemic disease and genocidal conflicts of an unprecedented magnitude. That, of course, is population control.

Whether population control is achievable by common consent; whether we will wait until it is forced upon us by a well-intentioned but unbending authority, or whether we will do nothing and suffer the consequences of an almighty population crash, is a matter of great concern. If we are as intelligent as we like to think that we are, surely we should be able to convince ourselves of the necessity to limit our numbers, and to find some acceptable and humane way to achieve this. But from where can the guidance and the leadership that is now so urgently needed come?

The traditional means by which the elders of societies established codes of conduct necessary for the community's health and well-being was to persuade the tribal priests to declare a divine decree supportive of the remedy. That device would now be a difficult strategy to employ. That is partly because of a widespread disbelief in a divine authority that could issues such edicts, and partly because the differing dogmas of different faiths would surely obstruct the formulation of an agreed theological reconstruction. In a world still plagued by religious antagonisms, there would seem to be no possibility that religious leaders will be able to act together to guide us through the travails that lie ahead.

This is a depressing conclusion, and I would delighted if, by their concerted and sustained influences for good, the world's theological leaders should prove me wrong. A simple humanistic philosophy, if only it could become widely adopted, might just be able to provide the necessary unification. The only dogma of humanism, as I understand it, is the reasonable, although unprovable, assumption that the consciousness of all other human beings is very much like one's own, with the same range of emotions and experiences extending from great happiness and to the depths of despair and unbearable pain. On that simple assumption it is reasonable not to want to cause unnecessary pain and suffering to anyone else, much as one hopes that none will cause pain and suffering to oneself. That simple assumption, universally shared, may be all that is needed to make universal benevolence the rule rather than the exception. I would like to believe in that possibility, but I fear that I am dreaming.

Quo Vadis

The American poet Robert Frost once indicated that where the path divided he always took the one least trod – and that, he said, had made all the difference. That interesting comment might well be applied prospectively rather than retrospectively to the progress of humanity. We can choose the one pathway by which we allow ourselves to be driven thoughtlessly towards ultimate disaster, as our genes dictate, or we can choose to temper the proliferation of the human species, and our attitudes towards each other, and possibly thereby to avert that disaster.

The path that mankind treads most frequently and easily is that of the animals generally: we breed excessively, we care only for ourselves, and we fight for what we need, careless of the consequences to others perceived as competitors or enemies. Our numbers always rise to the limit the food supply allows where it is checked by the premature deaths of those unable to find enough food to keep them alive. For the more fortunate of us, the passage through life is rendered less rough by privileged access to the fruits of the applied sciences of medicine and agriculture. Even if we ruthlessly protect these privileges, it is an illusion to belief that we can remain for ever insulated from the realities of life for others less fortunate. Hunger, disease and intertribal conflicts have remained the principal instruments by which our numbers are kept in harmony with the food supply. Those who cannot be adequately fed, and must watch their progeny and kinsfolk die prematurely, will, when they can, follow their instincts for survival and fight for a bigger share of the sunshine. As food production has been increased, and as the human population has increased in response, the proportion of the total mass of humanity condemned to hunger and premature death seems not to have changed greatly. Twenty per cent may be a fair assessment, and 20% of the present 6,000 million is 1,200 million hungry human beings facing a painful and early demise. That is more than the total population of the world only 200 years ago. For so long as birth rates remain in excess of the number that can be supported into adulthood, hunger of such magnitude will also remain, no matter what progress is made in agricultural productivity and medical deferment of death. If the 'have nots' acquire the means to get even with 'the haves', that would be the instinctive thing to do. In the meanwhile, those who protest the sanctity of human life should meditate for a while on what that actually means in terms of hunger, misery and premature death.

The alternative path through the history of a species, the one least trod, is that which only our own species could choose to take. That is because Homo sapiens alone has the mental faculty that enables it to survey the possible routes into the future, to assess their relative advantages and disadvantages, and then to direct itself accordingly. It has long been evident that some curb on the human procreative potential is the only way by which mankind can be spared the pains and consequences of the natural culling process by which animal populations are controlled. The advantages of electing to keep the human population of the world at that level at which all can be fed, and sustainably so, are i) that the risk of a major population crash is thereby greatly diminished; ii) that the anguish and suffering of natural population control by hunger and premature death could be largely eliminated, and iii) that intertribal fighting over food need no longer be imperative for survival. The disadvantage in electing that path into the future is that it would seem to require a greater degree of objective thinking and reasoning than many of us are capable of, or are prepared to attempt. Our inherited animal instincts to procreate and then to selectively protect our own progeny are powerful, and difficult to suppress, but possibly that could be done.

Most of us are persuaded, by a mixture of common sense and enforcement, to forego the freedom to freely choose which side of the road we drive along. This is because it is manifestly safest to do so, and therefore it is in one's own interest to conform to an agreed behaviour pattern. Likewise, most of us try to make a success of monogamy, which is not wholly consistent with our natures, because to do so has both biological and social benefits which outweigh the frustrations. Thus by a process of reasoning, conditioning and, perhaps, some degree of compulsion, it should be possible to make family limitation more generally practised than at present.

Population control no longer requires the sexual abstinence that Malthus was compelled to advocate. The only reasons, it would seem, for insisting on the pathway of uncontrolled population growth, and all the hazards and misery of that are i) ignorance of the consequences to humanity at large, ii) inadequate access to means of birth control; iii) adherence to theological indoctrinations that forbid most of the more reliable means of birth control or iv) a personal wish for a large family. Ignorance and inadequate means of birth control could be readily addressed on a worldwide scale, once the need to do so is sufficiently widely recognised. An enforced embargo on the right of individual couples to have a large family, if personal social and economic circumstances otherwise allow, may seem to be neither appropriate nor desirable. Unless, however, only a few couples choose to exercise the option of a large family, it will have an adverse effect on human welfare globally. To insist on that right in a world in which up to half the population is undernourished to some degree, could be considered both irresponsible and selfish. Thus economic or other pressures to discourage large families might well be deemed necessary in some circumstances. This could be effected by taxation disincentives.

The choice, for humanity at large, is summarised in Fig. 9.2. If the population is allowed to increase during the twenty-first century as is predicted by demographers (Fig. 9.2A), the gamble is whether sufficient food can be produced for 9,000 million human beings to exist concurrently and to be fed adequately. If it can be, then the world population might increase to that extent and then stabilise as the demographers anticipate that it will. Assuming that forecast is correct, the question that arises is, 'What will be the stabilising force?' It could be an enhanced incidence of premature mortality amongst those who cannot be adequately fed, or it could be effected by the wilful control of the birth rate such that hunger and early death is an unnecessary fate. There is no other way.

The next question is whether food production is enough to support 9,000 million will be sustainable. If not, a population crash would then be inevitable (Fig. 9.2C and D). Even, however, if that does not occur the maintenance of the population at that elevated level could still be only by the premature deaths of the 'surplus' progeny, or by birth control. Whether this population limitation is effected by the painful means of premature deaths of surplus progeny, or by the humane and painless means of planned birth control, is for us to decide. We are now where the path divides. *Quo vadis?* Where are you going?

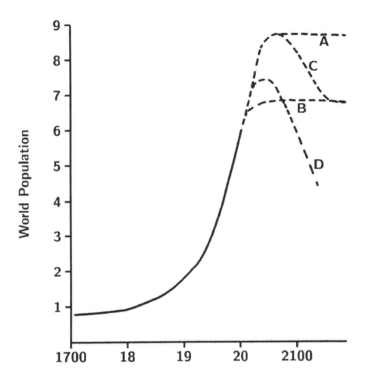

FIG. 9.2   THE CHANGE IN WORLD POPULATION BETWEEN THE END OF THE
SEVENTEENTH CENTURY AND THE END OF THE TWENTIETH CENTURY,
AND THE POSSIBLE CAUSES OF FURTHER CHANGES DEPENDING ON
CIRCUMSTANCES (BROKEN LINES): A IS THE DEMOGRAPHIC PREDICTION
THAT THE POPULATION WILL RISE TO 9 BILLION AND THEN STABILISE
WITHIN THE TWENTY-FIRST CENTURY; B IS IF THE SUSTAINABLE LEVEL OF
FOOD PRODUCTION ALLOWS ONLY A SMALLER BUT SUSTAINABLE RISE IN
POPULATION; C IS IF THE POPULATION RISES TO 9 BILLION, BUT THE
INCREASE IN FOOD PRODUCTION CANNOT BE SUSTAINED, AND THE
POPULATION DECLINES TO WHATEVER LEVEL CAN BE FED SUSTAINABLY,
AND D IS IF THE POPULATION INCREASES AS PREDICTED, BUT THE
OVERSTRESSED PRODUCTION OF FOOD FALLS AND PRECIPITATES A MAJOR
POPULATION CRASH. D COULD ALSO BE THE CONSEQUENCE OF A
HUNGER-DRIVEN,   TRIBAL-DRIVEN,   ECONOMICALLY-DRIVER   OR
THEOLOGICALLY-DRIVEN   NUCLEAR,   CHEMICAL   OR   BIOLOGICAL
WARFARE.

Chapter Ten

PRESCRIPTS BY OTHERS, AND A POSTSCRIPT

Pertinent Prescripts

Lucretius (95–55 BCE): 'Mankind obeys natural laws, like all the rest of Nature.'

Adam Smith (1776): 'Every species of animal naturally multiplies in proportion to the means of their subsistence, and no species can ever multiply beyond it. But in a civilised society it is only among the inferior ranks of people that the scantiness of subsistence can set limits to the further multiplication of the human species, and it can do so in no way than by destroying a great part of the children which their fruitful marriages produce.'

'Poverty does not discourage procreative activities but is extremely unfavourable to the rearing of children... In some places one half of the children die before they are seven, and in almost all places before they are nine or ten.'

Thomas Malthus (1798): 'Elevated as man is, above all other animals by his intellectual faculties, it is not to be supposed that the physical laws to which he is subjected should be essentially different from those which are observed to prevail in other parts of animated nature.'

'The perpetual tendency in the race of man to increase beyond the means of subsistence is one of the general laws of animated nature, which we have no reason to expect will change.'

'It is an obvious truth, which has been taken notice of by many writers, that population must always be kept down to the level of the means of subsistence.'

'It follows necessarily that the average rate of the actual increase of population over the greatest part of the globe, obeying the same laws as the increase of food, must be of a totally different character from the rate at which it would increase if unchecked. The great question which remains to be considered is the manner in which this constant and necessary check upon population practically operates.'

'Where population has increased nearly to the utmost limits of the food, all the preventative checks and the positive checks will naturally operate with increased force... till the population is sunk below the level of the food; and then the return to comparative plenty will again produce an increase, and after a certain period its further progress will again be checked by the same causes.'

'All these checks' [described by Flew as "the Unholy Trinity of War, Pestilence and Famine"] 'may be fairly resolved into misery and vice.'

'...this constantly subsisting cause of period misery has existed ever since we have had any histories of mankind, does exist at present, and will for ever continue to exist, unless some decided change take place in the physical constitution of our nature.'

'The great check on human population is an inevitable law of nature... The only enquiry that remains is, how it may take place with the least possible prejudice to the virtue and happiness of human society.'

'No possible good can arise from any endeavours to slur it over, or keep it in the background. On the contrary, the most baleful mischief may be expected from the unmanly conduct of not daring to face the truth, because it is unpleasant.'

Charles Darwin (1872): 'A struggle for existence inevitably follows from the high rate at which all organic beings tend to increase. Every being, which during its natural lifetime produces several eggs or seeds, must suffer destruction during some period of its life, and during some season or occasional year, otherwise, on the principal if geometric increase, its numbers would quickly become so inordinately great that no country could support the product. Hence, as more individuals are produced than can possibly survive, there must in every case be a struggle for existence, either with another of the same species, or with the individuals of distinct species, or with the physical conditions of life. It is the doctrine of Malthus applied with manifold force for the whole animal and vegetable kingdoms; for in this case there can be no artificial increase of food, and no prudential restraint from marriage. Although some species may be now increasing, more or less rapidly, in numbers, all cannot do so, for the world would not hold them.

There is no exception to the rule that every organic being naturally increases at so high a rate, that if not destroyed, the earth would soon be covered by the progeny of a single pair. Even slow-breeding man has doubled in twenty-five years, and at this rate, in a few thousand years there would literally be no standing room for his progeny.'

W E Hickson (1849, cited by Petersen, 1979): 'Malthus's theory does not admit of the slightest prospect of any permanent improvement in the mass of the people from the progress of temperance, thrift, industry, intelligence, and skill... unless coupled with the condition of fewer marriages than at present, or with artificial means taken to reduce the average number of births to a marriage.'

John Boyd Orr (1948): 'We have the knowledge. Have we got the common sense? Have we got the decency? Have we got the moral purpose to welcome the light which science and learning has given us? Or will imperialistic ambitious selfish interest, the unwillingness of people to make any sacrifice to the common good; will these decide the issue? If so the condemnation of our generation will be that light has come into the world and we have chosen darkness rather than light.'

'Hunger is the greatest of all politicians. Hungry mobs do not care "two hoots" about political theories; they will tear down any government which cannot provide food and will follow any demagogue who promises it.'

Charles Galton Darwin (1952): 'The human race, for its survival, must understand the limits to which it will always be subject. There can be no hope of either a great increase in food supply or of a planned and sustained restriction of world population. It will only be held down by recurrent periods of starvation. Malthus was right. There is no alternative to competitive struggle and marginal starvation, mocking the dignity of man. The Earth is finite and agriculture can only be much improved at high cost. No world authority or creed can long overcome these biological facts. Starvation will be the master.'

Max Nicholson (1954): 'Population rise cannot be halted by charity. One way or another the brake must be applied. The only questions are "how?" and "when?". We need not despair of mankind solving this problem if it is plainly and soberly stated and action is taken before it is too late to avert a major catastrophe. Death control must be matched with birth control.'

'It may not prove practical and if practicable it may not prove acceptable. Time will show. But given world population trends, is it defensible to shower money on research for preventing deaths, and also for hydrogen bombs, but assiduously to neglect research which might, in time, help to prevent world tensions from becoming uncontrollable and hydrogen bombs from being used.'

Gerald Durrell (1972): 'By our thoughtlessness, our greed and our stupidity we will have created, within the next fifty years or perhaps even less, a biological situation whereby we will find it difficult to live in the world at all. We are breeding like rats and this population explosion must be halted in some way. All religious factions, all political factions, and the government of the world, must face the facts, for if we persist in ignoring them, then, breeding like rats, we will have to die like them also.'

Richard Dawkins (1995): 'As I write thousands of all kinds are dying of starvation, thirst and disease. It must be so. If there is ever a time of plenty, this very fact will automatically lead to an increase in population until the natural state of starvation and misery is restored.'

D C Dennett (1995): 'As soon as something gets into the business of self-preservation, boundaries become important, for if you are setting out to preserve yourself, you don't want to squander effort trying to preserve the whole world: you draw the line.'

Lester Brown (1998): 'In effect, we are behaving as though we have no children, as though there will not be a next generation.'

Thoraya Obaid (2002): 'If we do not slow population growth, you're only going to increase the number of people who are under the poverty line, who are frustrated, who have no employment, no future. Right now 60 percent of the population in developing countries is under the age of 24. And these people are caught in a vicious circle of poverty where employment is not there, education is not there – *livelihood* is not there. And, therefore, you are building up more frustration, which eventually becomes a security issue. We should think ahead about the issues we are facing right now.'

David Attenborough (2003): 'If we do not take charge of our population size then nature will do it for us, and it is the poor people in the world who will suffer the most.'

A Postscript: Johannesburg, 2002

Shortly before the Johannesburg Summit on the state of the world Kofi Annan, Secretary General to the United Nations Organisation, wrote (in *State of the World 2002*):

> It is too late for the Summit to avoid the conclusion that there is a gap between the goals and promises set out in Rio [Rio de Janeiro, 1992] and the daily reality in rich and poor countries alike, but it is not too late to set the transformation more convincingly in motion.

The concern in Johannesburg in 2002 was to seek international agreement on, and commitment to, the appropriate steps that now need to be taken to alleviate humanity's multiplex distresses. The politicians, the economists, the theologians, and even the scientists, viewing the world from their various disintegrated narrow-angled viewpoints, made differing diagnoses, and advocated different therapies. Most of them are prescriptions for the alleviation of particular symptoms, rather than attempts to arrest the underlying causation of a sorely troubled world. For any prospect of the effective treatment of the basic ill, this must first be recognised, and discussed without any 'no-go' areas. That basic causation is, of course, the sheer mass of humanity that now burdens the world. Whether the immediate crisis in the state of human affairs is hunger on a now massive scale; inadequate drinking water and sanitation; the lack of decent housing, the toxic consequences of environmental pollution, or intra- and intertribal belligerency, it is the unnaturally inflated, and still growing, human population of the world, that is the root cause of them all. It follows, therefore, that attempts to relief the secondary orders of human distress can be little more than palliative unless urgent steps are taken to halt the rise in the human population. The often unratified, and mostly unenforceable, promises of the economically advantaged nations to seek a more equitable distribution of food, to assist in the drilling of water wells, and to generate trading opportunities, are all valid as minor gestures and contributions to human well-being if followed through. They do not, however, address the basic ill.

As was recognised by Thomas Malthus more than 200 years ago, populations will always expand to beyond the upper limit of what the available food supply can support, and will be held at that upper limit by the premature death of the inadequately fed. This is general to the animal kingdom, and Homo sapiens enjoys no natural immunity. What it could enjoy, if it so chose, is the unnatural immunity, which deliberate population limitation, could provide.

The diagnosis of the root cause of the problems that beset so much of mankind was not on the Johannesburg agenda. Consequently the only surely effective therapy remained unsought and unprescribed. This is all but incredible, and must have an explanation. A possible one was offered by Paul Brown (2002) before the Johannesburg Earth Conference had even assembled. He wrote:

> Although population remains a key issue, talk of controlling population will again be taboo in Johannesburg. A new coalition between the Vatican, Islamic states and Christian fundamentalists in the US, who have the ear of President Bush, will see to that.

This sounds like a conspiracy theory, and so far as I know there is no supporting documentary evidence of such a contract, but that is no proof that there was none. What is now evident is that whatever the reason, there was no serious and urgent discussion of population at the Johannesburg conference.

The tragedy of this failure is not just that premature mortality, preceded by hunger, is continuing to increase as the world's human population increases, but that the horror of mass hunger will surely be magnified by the horrors of the wars that mass hunger gives rise to. One does not die of hunger passively if fighting for food is even remotely likely to succeed. This basic animal instinct for aggressive self-preservation, is more ominous when it becomes a tribal endeavour; and intertribal conflicts have become progressively more so as the evolved intellect of the human species has created ever more devastating weapons of war. There are other reasons for human conflicts – lust for power, economic and material advantages, and religious intolerance being foremost – but the struggle for sustenance enough to survive will always provide the strongest motivation for so long as there is competition for food supply. The competition will continue for so long as our animal instinct to breed to excess remains untempered.

From what was achieved, or not achieved at Johannesburg, it seems very likely that if a third international attempt to reduce the gap between the 'haves' and the 'have nots' is made in, say, another ten years time, any pre-conference comment of the then UN Secretary General could be much the same as that of Kofi Annan. By then, however, it may well be too late for any effective action to change the course on which humanity is evidently set. If again dogma is allowed to triumph over reason, and nothing is done by mankind to halt 'the population explosion' (see Ehrlich and Ehrlich, 1991), nature will do it for us, as it does with any other animal species, but with a difference: Homo sapiens now has the ability to self-destruct.

Is it really already too late to bring mankind to its senses? Are our natural instinct too powerful to be tempered, even to spare ourselves from disaster? Can the human intellect, which was forged perhaps for personal survival in a competitive ecosystem, be re-applied to save ourselves now that we have made belligerency too dangerous? In theory, at least, we have the choice of lowering the competitive pressure ourselves by harnessing our natures, or of leaving Nature to takes its course. I hope; and I fear...

BIBLIOGRAPHY

Abramovitz, J N, 'Averting unnatural disasters', *State of the World 2001*, eds. L R Brown, C Flavin and H French, Norton, New York, 2001, pp.123–142

Annan, K A, 'Foreword', *State of the World 2002*, eds. C Flavin, S Dunn and A P McGinn, Norton, New York, 2002, pp.xix–xxii

Arrhenius, S, 'On the Influence of Carbonic Acid in the Air upon the Temperature of the Ground', *The London, Edinburgh and Dublin Philosophical Magazine and Journal of Science*, fifth series, 1886, pp.237–276

Attenborough, D, *Sunday Times*, London, 3 August 2003

Bacon, F, *The Advancement of Learning*, 1605

Balding, F, an editor of Malthus's first essay (cited by Flew, 1970)

Bentham, J, *Principles of Morals and Legislation*, 1789

Black, E, *War Against the Weak: Eugenics and America's Campaign to Create a Master Race*, Turnaround, 2004

Bonar, J, *Malthus and his Work,* second edn, Allen and Unwin, 1924

Boulding, K, *Malthus on Population*, University of Chicago, 1959

Brown, L R, *Who Will Feed China?,* Norton, New York, 1995

Brown, —, *State of the World*, Worldwatch Institute, Norton, New York, 1998

Brown, — and H Kane, *Full House: Reassessing the Earth's Population Carrying Capacity,* Norton, New York, 1994

Brown, P, 'Population', in *Earth* (supplement to *The Guardian*), London, 2002, pp.48–49

Cincotta, R P, R Engelman, and D Anastasion, *The Security Demographic,* Population Action International, Washington DC, 2003

Darwin, C, *The Origin of Species by Means of Natural Selection, or the Preservation of favoured species in the struggle for life*, Murray, London, 1859

——, C, *The Descent of Man and Selection in Relation to Sex,* Murray, London, 1871

Darwin, C G, *The Next Million Years,* Hart-Davis, 1952

Dawkins, R, *River out of Eden,* Harper Collins, New York, 1959

Dennett, D C, *Darwin's Dangerous Idea*, Simon and Schuster, New York, 1995

Durrell, G, *Catch Me a Colobus*, Harper Collins, 1972

Ehrlich, P and A Ehrlich, *The Population Explosion,* Simon and Schuster (Arrow Books), New York, 1991

Engels, F, *Outlines of a Critique of Political Economy* (1844) (cited by Flew, 1970, p.199)

——, F, Letter to Kautsky, 01 February 1881 (cited by Flew, 1970)

Evans, L T, *Feeding the Ten Billion,* CUP, Cambridge, 1998

Flavin, C and O Tunali, 'Climate of Hope: New Strategies for Stabilizing the World's Atmosphere', *Worldwatch*, Paper No.130, Worldwatch Institute, Washington, 1996

Flew, A, Introduction to the Pelican edition of *An Essay on the Principle of Population,* Penguin Books, Harmondsworth UK, 1970

Fourier, J, 'Remarques générales sur la temperature du globe terrestre et de espaces planetaires', *Annales de Chimie et de Physique,* 27, 1824, pp.136–167

Galton, F, *Hereditary Genius: An enquiry into its laws and consequences,* Appleton, New York, 1869

Halweil, B, 'Organic produce found to be higher in health-promoting Compounds', *Worldwatch,* 16 (4), 2003, p.25

Helleman, A, 'Consumer fears cancels European GM Research', *The Scientist,* 5 May 2003, pp.52–54

Hickson, W E, *Malthus: An Essay on the Principle of Population in Refutation of the Theory of the Rev. T R Malthus* (cited by Petersen, 1979), Taylor, Wilton and Maberly, London, 1849

Hitler, A, *Mein Kampf,* tr. J Murphy, Hutchinson, London, 1930

Huxley, A, 'The Double Crisis', *Food and People,* Publication 77, Bureau of Current Affairs, 1949

Jones, P D, and M E Mann, *Climate over past millennia, reviews of Geophysics,* 42 doi:10.1029/2003 RG 143, 2004

—, P D, M New, D E Parker, S Martin, and I G Rigor, *Surface Air Temperatures and its variations over the past 150 years, reviews of Geophysics,* 37, 1999, pp.173–199

Jordan, M, *The Encyclopedia of Gods,* Kyle Cathie, London, 1992

Lewis, W A, A background paper for a Duke of Edinburgh's Study Conference 2 (quoted by Flew, 1970), 54, OUP, Oxford, 1957

Lovelock, J, 'The Living Planet' (An interview report), *Nuclear Forum,* July 1992

Lucretius, *De rerum natura* (95–55 BCE), tr. Lucy Hutchinson, 1675

Lynas, M, 'At the end of our weather', in *Review* (a supplement to *The Observer*), London, 5 October 2003, pp.1–2

Malthus, T R (1798; 1830), *An Essay on the Principle of Population,* Penguin Books, Harmondsworth UK, 1970

Mann, M E, and P D Jones, 'Global surface temperatures over the past two millennia', *Geophysical Research Letters,* 30, 1820, 2003

Marr, A, *The Observer*, London, 6 September 1998, p.28

McEvedy, C and R Jones, *Atlas of World Population History*, Penguin Books, Harmondsworth UK, 1978

McFadden, J, 'Sowing the seeds of a better future: Ignore the doubters. GM crops can help to feed the world', *The Guardian*, London, 4 April 2002

Meacher, M, Quoted from *The Ecologist* by *New Scientist*, 8 March 2003

Nicholson, M, 'A brake on births', *The Observer*, London, 29 August 1954

Obaid, T, *Worldwatch*, 15 (5), 2002, pp.36–37

Orr, J, Boyd, 'Food – the Foundation of World Unity', National Peace Council pamphlet: *Towards world Government No.1,* 1948

Pearson, K, *National Life from the Standpoint of Science*, second edn, Cambridge University Press, Cambridge, 1919

Petersen, W, *Malthus*, Heinemann, London, 1979

Russell, J, 'The Way Out?', *Food and People*, Publication 77, Bureau of Current Affairs, 1949

Ryan, F, *Tuberculosis: The Greatest Story Never Told*, Swift Publishers, UK, 1992

Smith, A, *An Enquiry into the Nature and Causes of The Wealth of Nations*, 1776

Stott, P, 'You can't control the climate', *New Scientist*, 2 November 2003, p.25

Titmuss, T M, 'Problems of Population. Association for the Education in Citizenship', discussion Handbook No.9, English University Press, London, 1942

UN Intergovernmental Panel on Climate Change, 1995

State of the World, Worldwatch Institute, Norton, New York (Revised each year)

Vital Signs, Worldwatch Institute, Norton, New York (Published every year or every other year)

29513731R00128

Printed in Great Britain
by Amazon